Blogger's Quick Guide to Working with a Team

THE ULTIMATE GUIDE TO BLOGGING FASTER AND
BETTER WITH THE HELP OF OTHERS

Rebecca Livermore

Professional Content Creation

LITTLETON, COLORADO

Rebecca Livermore
Blogger's Quick Guide to Working with a Team

Learn more information at: www.ProfessionalContentCreation.com

What People Are Saying About Rebecca

If you're looking for someone that's incredibly honest, reliable, and loyal to the end, Rebecca Livermore fits the bill as well as anyone I've ever met. Frankly, I just feel extremely blessed to be on the same team with her. Marcus Sheridan, The Sales Lion

If you want to streamline your business, you must leverage pieces of your business you know will hit the mark every single time. That's why I work with Rebecca. -- Amy Porterfield, Social Media Strategist, Co-author of *Facebook Marketing All-in-One for Dummies*

Rebecca is an excellent communicator. She is proactive and diligent, volunteering ideas and creative solutions to problems. I highly recommend her. -- Michael Hyatt, New York Times Bestselling Author

Rebecca brings tremendous value to any project, but she is especially gifted with words -- written and spoken. She is a great editor, producer and ally. Plus she always delivers above and beyond results. Glad to have worked with her and highly recommend her. Phil Mershon, Director of Events at Social Media Examiner

Rebecca is a joy to work with. Her personal demeanor, coupled with her strikingly strong work ethic is exactly what attracts me to her as a professional service provider over and over again. Chris Ducker, Virtual CEO, Serial Entrepreneur, Keynote Speaker, Bestselling Author, Blogger, Podcaster.

Rebecca is an amazing communicator. Honest, professional, and always a delight to talk to — both in person and over email. She always looks ahead for her clients and goes above and beyond to make things even better, without the other person having to ask for it. I

Rebecca Livermore

would definitely recommend Rebecca and her team at Professional Content Creation. Pat Flynn, Smart Passive Income Podcast and Blog

Rebecca has a rare sensitivity to other people and consistently manages to encourage and inspire them. Her words are always well chosen and her style gracious and uncluttered. Clark Cothern, Senior Pastor at Living Water Community Church, Ypsilanti, MI

Rebecca is an excellent team player as she keeps the big picture in view while diligently contributing to the tasks at hand. Rebecca's hard work, attention to detail, and encouragement of her colleagues makes it a pleasure to work with her. Jeff Denlinger, President, WorldVenture

Table of Contents

Rebecca Livermore

Rebecca Livermore

Rebecca Livermore

Foreword

CREATIVE FREEDOM. It's the reason you started blogging in the first place. It excites you to think the words you write can instantly be read by millions of people. Your words can have power, meaning and impact.

Your words can live on long after you're gone. We're the first generation since the beginning of time to leave a digital legacy. What you publish on your blog, record on a podcast, and share in a video can out last you. It's amazing to think that people around the world can be helped today from a blog post you published over four years ago.

Broken focus. It's what blocks your creative freedom. The day you launched your blog was the day your to do list grew to a million things. A million things that are all vying for your attention. Sure, many things on the list need to get done. The challenge is in choosing what you should do and what you should have other people do for you. Has the following ever happened to you?

In the midst of your busy schedule, a small window of opportunity opens up for you to work on your blog. For example's sake, let's say you have an hour to yourself before the next event on your calendar. Since you haven't published a blog post in over three weeks, you're determined to post something new before your time is up.

You open the laptop to find your email inbox open in front of you. Why not go ahead and check your email before you write that blog post? One of the emails informs you of a new video on YouTube you must watch, so you hop on over to watch the five-minute video. The video outlines a social media posting strategy you would love to implement and so you write it down on your to do list.

You then remember that it's been awhile since you checked your social media accounts. You hop over and spend time on Facebook, Twitter, LinkedIn, Pinterest and others. Another fifteen minutes has gone by but at least you feel a bit better that you posted new content on your social media outlets.

Back to your email you discover a customer needs help resetting their password for your online course. Since you desire to have amazing customer service, you decide to do it yourself, right now. This takes another ten minutes of your time.

Let's cut this long scenario short. An hour goes by; you have yet to write one word of your blog post and you're frustrated wondering how you're going to get all of these things done.

We've all been there. More to do than the time we have available to do it. We grow frustrated when we see other more successful bloggers who seem to get everything done in an effortless way. They must be more productive we think. So, we decide to beat ourselves into submission and be more disciplined. That lasts for half a day before everything becomes unraveled.

But what if I told you there was a better way? In a *Blogger's Quick Guide to Working with a Team*, Rebecca Livermore lays out a comprehensive plan on how you can go further, faster by building a team. I know what you are thinking. "I just can't afford to hire a team." Before you buy into that limiting belief, I want to encourage you to read ahead. Rebecca has laid out both free and affordable ways to get more done through teams.

I want to challenge you to identify one important task and outsource it using one of Rebecca's recommendations within the next two weeks. It's important that you keep taking tiny steps when outsourcing. When it comes to building a team, it's not something you go into, it's something you grow into. Start growing an amazing team today.

Jonathan Milligan
BloggingYourPassion.com

My Gift to You

As a thank you for purchasing this book, I want to give you my eCourse, The Five Secrets to Developing the Blogging Habit absolutely free!

To get your complimentary eCourse delivered right to your inbox all you have to do is click here or visit http://professionalcontentcreation.com/blogginghabit

Rebecca Livermore

Introduction

THE FACT THAT YOU'RE READING THIS BOOK leads me to believe that you're a blogger or at the very minimum are considering starting a blog.

Perhaps blogging isn't all you thought it would be, and chances are you've found it difficult (to put it mildly). Or maybe you've put off starting a blog because you're worried about how much work it will be. At the same time, for various reasons you may feel resistance when it comes to taking on team members.

In spite of any resistance you may feel, you're holding this book (or your eReader!) in your hands for a purpose.

BUILD A BETTER BLOG WITH THE HELP OF A TEAM

Imagine what it would be like to no longer have to do everything yourself.

What if instead of trying to do it all (and dreading many of the things on your to-do list!), if when you sat down to work on your blog, you had a sense of satisfaction and (dare I say it?) even joy?

What if you could hand tasks to skillful people who love doing them, rather than doing a crappy job on them yourself? (Let's face it, nobody is good at everything!)

The good news is, even if you have a super limited budget, getting the help you need to build a successful blog is within your reach. It's possible without selling off your first born or resorting to eating nothing but mac'n cheese!

THE MINIMUM EFFECTIVE DOSE

I first heard about the minimum effective dose through Tim Ferriss. The basic concept is that the minimum effective dose is the smallest amount of something that will achieve the desired result and that anything beyond that is wasteful.

An illustration that Tim uses to explain the concept is that water boils at 212 degrees Fahrenheit (100 degrees Celsius). You can raise the temperature beyond that, but regardless of how high you raise it, it will never be "more boiled." Boiled water is boiled water! Because of that, using a higher temperature is not only unnecessary, it's wasteful.

A LITTLE DAB WILL DO YA

Let's look at this another way. In the 50s and 60s, Brylcream, a popular men's styling gel, had a catchy jingle that said, among other things, "a little dab will do ya." The idea was that there was no need for men to slather the goop on their hair for it to be effective – a little dab was all that you needed.

NO EMPLOYEES (OR OFFICE SPACE) NECESSARY

A lot of people fear that to grow a blog with the help of a team that they'll need to hire employees, and perhaps even go as far as to rent office space.

While there's nothing wrong with hiring employees and renting office space, the good news is, for most bloggers, "a little dab will do ya." Chances are, formal employees and office space are unnecessary.

The goal of this book is to help bloggers find the minimum effective dose (or "little dab") when it comes to working with a team – and applying just enough that's needed -- to have maximum results.

Rebecca Livermore
ABOUT THE AUTHOR

Bestselling author Rebecca Livermore knows better than most how to build a blog with the help of a team.

Not only does she run a successful blog with assistance from her own team members, prior to launching out on her own, she worked for top bloggers such as Michael Hyatt, Amy Porterfield, Pat Flynn and Marcus Sheridan. She knows firsthand what it's like to be a team member and what it's like to manage team members of her own.

Her unique perspective will help you grow a strong and healthy team that will not only work for you, but that will help you nurture team loyalty from your blogging dream team.

ABOUT THIS BOOK

This book is built on the premise that even bloggers that aren't making mega bucks blogging can afford to have a team. As you read through the following pages, you'll discover how to grow a team on a limited budget, including low-cost and in some cases even free ways to get great team members.

You'll also get a grasp on:

*How doing everything yourself can cost you more money than hiring others to do the work

*How to know when you're ready to hire team members

*Four free ethical and positive ways to leverage your relationships with others

*Where and how to hire your first team members

*The best ways to share files and passwords with team members

*Tips for keeping the channels of communication wide open

*How to manage your team when it's small and how to transition your management as your blog and business grow

*The best ways to maintain loyalty and the overall happiness of your team members

*and what to do when things go wrong (because, unfortunately, sometimes they will!)

Since you're reading this book, I'll wager a bet that you're a busy person, so let's not dawdle. It's time to dive in, and learn how you can blog faster and better with the help of a team!

Rebecca Livermore

Why Bloggers Should Build a Team

The nice thing about teamwork is that you always have others on your side. ~Margaret Carty

PERHAPS YOU'RE NOT QUITE CONVINCED that building a team for your blog is the best thing to do. That's okay; I've been there myself!

In fact, I've always been somewhat of a DIY type of person. Even as a little child, I strove to find ways to do things myself. I'm not sure why I've always been hesitant to ask for help when I need it, and to be honest, it's been a hard habit for me to break, and yet breaking the habit has been worth the effort!

In this section of the book we'll take a look at:

*Common reasons bloggers don't want to take on team members

*3 ways people make me a better blogger

*The importance of accountability

Rebecca Livermore

   *Hidden costs of doing everything yourself

   *The value of playing to your strengths

   *How to create more content for your blog in less time

   *The types of things you should NOT outsource

Chapter 1

COMMON REASONS BLOGGERS DON'T WANT TEAM MEMBERS

Perhaps you'll be able to relate to some of the following common reasons many bloggers don't want to bring on team members. Some of them are ones that I've struggled with personally, and others are ones that I've heard from other bloggers.

HOW MUCH IS THIS GOING TO COST?!

One of the biggest concerns that bloggers have when it comes to outsourcing is the matter of money. This is especially true if you're just starting out as a blogger and not making much, or perhaps any money.

If money is one of your biggest concerns when it comes to growing your team, I have good news for you! In the coming chapters, I'll provide tips for evaluating your needs and setting a budget. I'll even give you low and believe it or not, NO cost ways of building a team.

I'LL DO IT MY WAY

Do you ever worry that if someone else does a task for you, that they won't do it, quite right? If so, as a true perfectionist, I hear ya!

It is hard to find people who will do things exactly the same way that you would do them. But I have good news for you: sometimes people you hire will actually do things BETTER than you could do them yourself. (Shocking, but true!)

In addition to that, if you want things done a specific way, that can be handled through proper training, and the creation of processes. You'll find tips on how to go about that in Chapter 28.

GOOD HELP IS HARD TO FIND

I know that it can be hard to find good people to help with your blog, but I also know that it can be well worth the effort! Trust me, there are good people out there who can provide you the help you need, without making you go broke. In Section 4 I provide tips on how to hire your first team members, and if you do happen to end up with a dud, I go over what to do when things go wrong in Section 9.

You may have some other reasons of your own as to why you don't want to hire help. My hope is that by reading this book you'll get over the hurdles that are keeping you from this important step in the life of your blog. ☺

Chapter 2

3 WAYS PEOPLE MAKE ME A BETTER BLOGGER

BLOGGING IS OFTEN A SOLITARY ENDEAVOR, but it doesn't have to be.

Now it's true that as I'm writing this book (and when I'm blogging), I'm sitting alone, and it would probably be hard for me to get it done if I was around other people. This is especially true for me since I don't concentrate well when there is a lot of noise and distractions around me.

> But apart from the solitary time that is necessary for the actual writing, as a blogger, I wouldn't be where I am today without people. And neither will you! Trust me, we all need people!

HERE ARE A JUST 3 WAYS THAT PEOPLE MAKE ME A BETTER

BLOGGER.

---

1. Feedback

Feedback is something that all people, including bloggers, need. Without feedback, it's hard to know whether or not you're hitting the mark.

> For example, someone may leave a comment on one of your blog posts, which makes it clear that something you wrote that you thought was obvious isn't obvious at all.

From that, you learn not to be blinded by the curse of knowledge [Ref 1] that so many bloggers experience.

Or you may find that your posts don't get as much engagement as you'd like, or that your opt-ins aren't converting as well as you had hoped. When I find myself in that position, I might ask my mastermind group for input, or hire someone to do a blog review.

Without feedback, you're left in the dark, trying to figure things out on your own. Not a fun (or productive) place to be!

---

2. Encouragement

Writers groups have been around for a long time, and nowadays we have options such as Facebook groups that bring bloggers from around the world together. Part of what happens in these groups is feedback, as mentioned in number one above, but another aspect is encouragement.

No one else understands some of the trials that bloggers go through in the same way that other bloggers do. When you spend time with other bloggers, you'll find that you're not alone in how you feel or what you're experiencing. No doubt, at least one of your blogging friends will be able to relate, and bring you some encouragement because of it.

---

3. Accountability

Today I pushed myself to finish a blog post, even though I felt like I didn't have time to do it and wasn't really in the mood to write. Why? Today was my weekly mastermind meeting, and I was going to have to report on how I did with my goals for the week. I share many of my blogging related goals with this group, and because of that, I'm far more likely to accomplish them.

Accountability doesn't make me a perfect blogger. Sometimes I still fail to meet my blogging goals. But accountability makes me a better blogger than I would be without it. I accomplish more as a blogger due to having others check on me and ask how I'm doing on a regular basis.

There are many other reasons why people make me a better blogger, but these three are the main ones.

> If you're trying to make it on your own as a blogger, stop. Yes, block out time alone to write, but be just as intentional about the relationships that can make you a better blogger.

Rebecca Livermore

Chapter 3

A DOUBLE DOSE OF ACCOUNTABILITY

I MENTIONED ACCOUNTABILITY in the previous chapter, but since accountability partners are such an important part of my team, I wanted to delve deeper into it. Why? Accountability helps people stay on track with many things, including blogging.

It's a pretty simple concept. The way that it works is to tell someone, or perhaps a small group of people, what you want to accomplish and by when. Then you have to give an account as to whether or not you did it. It's a positive version of peer pressure.

AN EXAMPLE OF MY OWN BLOG-RELATED ACCOUNTABILITY

I'm currently accountable to two people/groups for my content creation. One is my mastermind group. We meet weekly on Google Hangouts for our meeting. One small, but important part of our meeting is sharing our goals for the week, and reporting in on how we did on our goals from the previous week.

Another person that holds me accountable is my business mentor. We meet by phone, once a month. At the end of each call, I share what I want to accomplish before our next meeting, and then at the beginning of each call I share whether or not I met the last month's goal. Both of these relationships are vital to me and help me keep moving forward.

For example, one goal that I consistently share with my mastermind group is getting at least one blog post done each week. Our group meets at 2:00 p.m. every Thursday, and I often find myself pushing to get my post(s) for the week completed early on Thursday morning. Why? Because I don't want to have to tell them that I failed.

Those are both long-term relationships, but sometimes short-term relationships work as well. For example, I had "been meaning to" redo my videos for my Content Repurposing Made Easy course [Ref 2], and just couldn't ever seem to "find the time" to do it. When I received an email from a video coach about a 30-day video challenge, where I would be held accountable for meeting individual video production goals over a four-week period, I jumped on the opportunity. And it worked! I got the four videos that I committed to done before the challenge ended.

No doubt about it, as a human, sometimes I do fail to meet my goals. However, just knowing that I'm going to have to give an account for what I did or did not do moves me forward. It helps me to get more done than I would have without the accountability.

WHAT TO DO WHEN ACCOUNTABILITY DOESN'T WORK

It's important to note that my accountability relationships haven't always worked. There have been times when I've had an accountability partner who didn't follow through on keeping me accountable. For example, if I failed to meet my goals, she would mostly make excuses for me. She meant well, I'm sure, but that particular accountability relationship didn't last too long because it didn't help me move forward as needed.

You may experience something similar, and if so, move on until you find an accountability partner or group that helps you meet your blogging goals.

If possible find an accountability partner that you admire on a deep level, one that you won't want to let down. This can increase the "pressure" to meet your goals. A person or group that you respect but are not intimidated by is ideal.

TRY GOING PUBLIC

If you want to take things up a notch, try, going public with your blogging goals. When I say, "going public," I mean to do so in a big place, such as announcing your goal on your website or blog. When you do this, your goals become known by a larger group of people than a few trusted friends. It can increase the pressure (in a good way), to accomplish your blogging goals.

Rebecca Livermore

Chapter 4

THE HIGH COST OF DOING EVERYTHING YOURSELF

IN CHAPTER 1, *Common Reasons Bloggers Don't Want Team Members* I mentioned that one of the common reasons bloggers have for not building a team is the concern over how much it will cost. Trust me, I hear you on that one! I'm a solopreneur, which is pretty much the exact opposite of being a big corporation with deep pockets, and an operating budget that would make even Donald Trump blush. (If Donald Trump saw my budget, he'd probably laugh!)

To compound this, as of the beginning of this month, I let the last of my clients go. I did that so that I can devote 100% of my time to creating MY content. That's a great thing. BUT, what that means is that I no longer have ANY guaranteed income.

Because of this, more than ever before, I MUST pay attention to my budget. In spite of that, I regularly hire help for my blog. Why? Because the failure to do so can be incredibly expensive. Read on for the hidden costs of doing everything yourself.

WHEN A 15-MINUTE TASK BECOMES AN ALL-DAY EVENT

Have you ever spent all day (or at the very least, a couple of hours) trying to figure something out yourself? I have! In fact, sometimes in the quest to save a few bucks, I've spent all day watching tutorials on

Rebecca Livermore

Lynda.com. After trying and failing to get the desired results, I've given up and reached out to a professional.

To my chagrin, the pro turned around the completion of the task quicker than I could prepare and eat lunch. Not only did I waste a lot of time trying to get the darn thing done, in the end I ended up hiring someone to do it. And since the pro was incredibly skilled in the task and was able to complete it quickly, it didn't even cost me that much.

What did cost me was the fact that I let my desire to save money derail me from the tasks that I am skilled in, not to mention tasks that help to move my business forward.

If I had only hired someone right off rather than trying to do it myself, I would have saved myself a lot of time and frustration. I also would have avoided the next problem, the extra expense associated with someone else having to fix what I did.

CLEAN UP ON AISLE 9

Not only can you waste a lot of time trying to do something outside of your skillset, in the long run, it can cost you more than if you hired a professional in the first place.

For example, let's say that you decided to "tweak" your website yourself. It was just a little tweak, and you wanted it done right away, not to mention that you preferred not to spend money paying your web person to do it.

But somehow, when you were working on it, something went terribly wrong. And your website no longer looks, well, like your website. In a panic, you do what you should have done right from the start: reached out to your web developer.

> Since your site is now officially messed up, you need help, and you need it fast.

If you're anything like me, you may not know exactly what you did to mess things up. If that's the case, your web developer will have to figure out where things went wrong. Not only will this take more time than if you had just had her do the work in the first place, you might also have to pay a rush fee.

> The emergency you created can be expensive, and it could have been avoided had you just called a professional rather than trying to do it yourself.

HOW MUCH IS YOUR TIME REALLY WORTH?

What's your time worth? The answer to this question is different for everyone, and it's an incredibly important one to answer. If you provide services and charge an hourly rate, it's an easy question to answer. If you don't charge an hourly rate, you'll have to give this your best shot. Take a minute to think about it, before you read on.

GOT IT? NOW CONSIDER THIS:

> Every time you're tempted to do something yourself, consider whether or not someone can do it cheaper than you can. For example, if your hourly rate is $50, (which is rather low for many professionals), and you can hire someone for a lower hourly rate, then you should do so.

In this scenario, keep in mind the extra time it will take you to do something, compared to the professional you may hire. Using $50 an hour as an example, you may avoid asking your web developer, who charges $100 per hour for help. But if it would take her thirty minutes, and it would take you three hours to figure the thing out, it would cost you $50 to hire it out compared to $150 to do it yourself.

The math works even better if the person you hire is not only an expert at something but charges less than you do. For instance, again using your rate of $50 an hour as an example, why should you ever do something that you can pay a virtual assistant $25 an hour (or perhaps even less) to do?

The key thing to remember is that while it may seem that you save money by doing things yourself, you must consider the cost of your time. Sometimes the best way to increase your bottom line is to pay someone else to do the work for you.

EVEN THOUGH IT TAKES TIME. . .

Blogging can be a very profitable thing to do for your business. However, the payoff may not come for a long time. Because of that, it can be tempting to do everything yourself until your blog is bringing in the big bucks. I understand that, I really do. And I'm a bootstrapper at heart. But while you may need to use a little restraint when it comes to hiring help for your blog, before you dismiss the possibility, be sure to consider the hidden cost of doing everything yourself.

CREATE MORE CONTENT IN LESS TIME

Something that I've learned in my years as both a blogger and a content manager for other bloggers is that the more content that is created and the more consistent the content is published, the better the results.

Publishing content sporadically, or at a very low level will cost you from the perspective that your blog won't accomplish as much as it could.

One of the biggest problems of doing it all yourself is that you simply can't create as much content as you ideally should. I struggle with this myself, even though the bulk of my time is spent on content creation. The bottom line is that unless you're willing to hire help for your blog, the level of content that you are able to put out will be less. That will cost you when it comes to traffic to your blog, and the number of people who opt in to your email list. It may even cost you credibility, if doing it all yourself means that you're an inconsistent blogger.

Rebecca Livermore

Chapter 5

WHAT YOU SHOULDN'T OUTSOURCE

WHAT I 100% DO NOT RECOMMEND is hiring a ghost writer for your blog. What I mean by that is, don't hire someone to just create content for you from scratch, without your input, and slap your name on it. If you go that route, your content will lack your personality and expertise, and if people find out you're doing it, it will discredit you. You can, however, get around this with options such as Blogging Your Voice (explained in Chapter 22), but that only works because of the business owner's (e.g. YOUR) involvement in the process.

The bottom line is that if content bears your name, YOU need to be involved in it. This is why it's important for you to do the initial content creation, in whatever form you're best at, and then hire help from there.

PLAY TO YOUR STRENGTHS

It's always best to spend the bulk of your time doing what you do best.

Here's an example of how this works for me.

Rebecca Livermore

As a professional content creator, I feel at home when I'm creating content. Because of that, I create most of the content for my blog myself, and yet even I realize the value of hiring help for my blog.

Let's face it; blogging is a LOT of work. And most bloggers aren't sitting around wishing they had more to do, especially if blogging is just a part of the business rather than the business itself. And while I'm not a fan of business owners having a "hands off" approach to their content creation, that doesn't mean you can't outsource at least some of it.

When it comes to hiring help for your blog, I recommend creating the initial content yourself. You can hire other people to repurpose the content, edit and upload content, and enhance the content in other ways.

Even when it comes to content creation, you should always start with your strengths. Then let others do the things that either you aren't good at, don't like, or shouldn't be doing for one reason or another.

As an example, I'm a strong writer, so the base of all of my content is written, and I do 100% of that myself. From there, I can hire people to create videos, SlideShare presentations, infographics and so on based on the content I've already created.

You, on the other hand, may find that you love podcasting or video creation, but hate writing. If that's the case, you can first create your videos or podcasts, and have a writer create written content based on the other types of content you've created.

Focusing on creating content for your blog in a way that fits with your unique strengths and hiring others to do other tasks that you're not so great at is one of the biggest benefits of growing a team.

WHAT TO DO IF YOU CAN'T WRITE?

As mentioned above, playing to your strengths and letting others do everything else is a great way to maximize your blogging efforts.

At the same time, I feel that writing is an important aspect of blogging, especially since Google loves written content. Because of that, I think it's important to include written content as part of your blogging mix.

But what if you can't write? First let me say that many bloggers are not what would be considered good writers in a traditional sense. My friend and former client, Marcus Sheridan (a.k.a. The Sales Lion [Ref 3]) is a great example of this. He tends to use words like "ain't" and "dang," and one of his favorite words, is "crapola." None of these is considered great writing by grammar snobs.

The crazy thing is that his style of writing is what many people love about him, even though it's not perfect. When I worked for him, I proofread his posts and cleaned up his typos and major grammatical goofs, but kept his voice – and the majority of his words -- intact.

The point is, when it comes to hiring help for your writing, it doesn't have to be an all or nothing thing!

Rebecca Livermore

SECTION 2

Evaluating Needs

In Chapter 1, I covered the topic of people being afraid to hire a team because of how much it can cost. I'm not gonna lie – it CAN be expensive to have a team if your team is massive.

My question for you is, "Do you NEED a massive team?" Not only can massive teams be expensive, but they can also be a lot to manage.

Most likely if you're reading this book, you're not at the place of needing a massive team. The goal of this section is to help you determine exactly what you need to hire help for, and how to determine how much you should spend on your team.

SPECIFICALLY, WE'LL COVER:

    *How to Know When You're Ready to Hire a Team

    *The Three Lists of Freedom – a great exercise by Chris Ducker

    *Setting a Budget for Your Team

    *How to Determine Whether to Hire Part-Time, Temporary or Full-Time Help

Rebecca Livermore

Chapter 6

How to Know When You're Ready to Hire Help

I'M A FIRM BELIEVER IN HIRING HELP before you *desperately* need it. The reason for this is that if you wait until you're desperate, you may make a hasty decision, and instead of hiring the best person (or people) for the job.

In addition to that, it takes time to get new team members up to speed, and if you're already overwhelmed, you may find it difficult to find the time to get things in place for your new team members, not to mention the time it takes to train them.

Before You Can Afford It

It can be difficult to hire people when you first start your blog, especially since you likely won't be making much, if any money at the beginning.

However, ideally, you'll hire help before your blog is profitable. I'm not a big fan of debt, so I'm not talking about racking up credit card bills. However, at the beginning, you may need to pay for help for your blog from your personal accounts.

Before you protest too loudly, let me assure you that I'm not talking about personal sacrifices that require you to eat nothing but beans and rice, nor am I suggesting that you pull your kids out of their extracurricular activities, or that you take out a home equity loan.

What I am suggesting however, is that you look for small ways to get help for your blog early on. The reason for this is twofold. First, it will free you from the mindset that you need to do everything yourself. Second, it will give you more time to devote to actually building your blog in a way that will make it more profitable in the long run.

The great news is that you can start in very small ways. Five dollars here, twenty or thirty dollars there. Skip the pizza, and instead, hire someone to enter data into a spreadsheet, or create some images for your blog.

Obviously, if your budget can handle more than that, go for it! But the key is to start small, and work your way up.

SIGNS THAT IT'S TIME TO HIRE HELP

As I mentioned previously, you want to hire help before you're on the brink of a nervous breakdown. Here are some specific signs that it's time to move forward.

*You have tasks that you dread doing. In fact, you may not only dread doing them, they may sit there undone, because you simply can't get yourself to do them.

*Your customer service is not at the level that you'd like. Just to be clear, customer service goes beyond dealing with actual customers. For instance, I consider customer service to be replying to emails from blog visitors, email subscribers and so on. If you don't have time to reply to people who reach out to you, it may be time to hire help!

*If you took any time off, your blog and business would fall apart.

*You're too busy to take on new clients.

*You don't update your blog consistently because you never seem to have time to get around to it.

*Your family hardly ever sees you and when they do, you're in a bad mood.

Any other pressing things that bother you may also be an indication that it's time to hire help now, even if in a small way.

Rebecca Livermore

Chapter 7

3 Lists to Freedom

I FIRST HEARD ABOUT THE 3-LISTS TO FREEDOM [Ref 4] when I attended a 1-Day Business Breakthrough [Ref 5] event led by Pat Flynn and Chris Ducker. If you don't already know, Chris Ducker is the King of Outsourcing. (I'll write about his agency a bit later in this book, so stay tuned!)

At the event, each of the participants had 15-minutes to present a challenge in their business, and then Pat, Chris, and the other participants provided feedback.

I can't recall who or what prompted it, but at one point, Chris outlined his method for determining what to outsource. It was so good, everyone immediately started taking notes, and I know that many of the participants hired help for their business based on that list.

Below is a summary of the process to creating your personal 3 Lists to Freedom.

Superhero Syndrome

Are you trapped in your business? If so, it could be that you're suffering from what Chris calls, "Superhero Syndrome."

The basic idea behind Superhero Syndrome is that if you work hard enough, you simply can't be defeated.

Unfortunately, nothing could be further from the truth. In Chapter 1, I went over some of the hang ups that bloggers have about hiring help, and how to look at those things in a healthier manner.

But one thing I didn't address is a very important thing that Chris addresses, and that is, burnout. If you try to do everything yourself, while you may be able to sustain it for a short period of time, eventually, you'll burn out.

If you have this tendency, trust me, you're not alone!

One of the biggest complaints Chris hears from business owners is that there isn't enough time to do the things they need to do. As business owners, it's important to understand that time is your most valuable commodity. While you can always generate more money, you can never generate more time. Once you use it, it's gone. Forever.

Because of this, as business owners, we need to make sure that the way we spend our time is most beneficial for our business.

This exercise will change how you look at your business.

SHARPEN YOUR PENCIL!

To do this exercise, you don't need a whole lot. Are you ready? Let's get started!

First, grab a pen and a piece of paper.

Second, draw two lines down the middle. You'll end up with three columns.

#1: In the first column, write down all of the things you simply hate doing on a day-by day basis. These are the things you simply can't stand! If you're like me, these are the things that you tend to procrastinate on!

#2: In the second column, write down the things you can't do yourself. They are things that you struggle with. For example, it could be developing a website or creating a logo, etc. The bottom line is these are the things you simply don't have the skill to do. You may not be able to do them at all, or you may be able to do them, but not very well.

#3: In the third column, write down the things you feel that as a business owner you shouldn't be doing on a day-to-day basis.

Now it's important to understand, you may be good at these things. You may even like doing them. But even if you like doing them, and are good at them, that doesn't mean you should do them yourself.

These are the tasks that aren't the most profitable ones for you to do, things that CAN be done by other people who can do them for less than what your time is worth.

Don't Procrastinate

If at all possible, don't put this exercise off until a "better time." Do it now. It's that important!

By the way, if you're not a pen and paper kind of person, do this on your computer. Simply open a Word or Google Doc, and create a table with three columns.

Or if you're away from your computer, pull out your smart phone or tablet and use whatever app you have that will allow you to jot these things down. It doesn't have to be pretty. The important thing is to make note of these things while they're fresh on your mind.

Really, do it now. You'll be glad you did.

Rebecca Livermore

Chapter 8

SETTING A BUDGET

WHILE I CAN'T TELL YOU EXACTLY how much you should budget for help for your blog, in this chapter I'm going to provide some basic principles that will help you determine how much of your money you should allocate for outsourcing.

PROFIT FIRST

One of the best business books that I've read in a long time is *Profit First* [Ref 6] by Mike Michalowicz.

The basic premise is that you pay profits first, and whatever is left is available for your expenses. This is the exact opposite of what most business owners do – paying expenses first. The idea is that your expenses will expand to the amount of money you have. If you see a balance in your bank account, you may spend it, simply because it's there.

With the Profit First method, when money comes in, you immediately allocate it to the appropriate accounts.

Here's the suggested breakdown, along with the recommended percentages:

Rebecca Livermore
   *Profit: 5%
   *Taxes: 15%
   *Owner's Pay: 50%
   *Operating Expenses: 30%

To make this easier to understand, I'll start with a nice round number, $1,000. For every thousand dollars that comes in, here's how you'd allocate it, according to the above percentages:

   *$50 would go into your Profit Account
   *$150 would go into your Tax Account
   *$500 would go into your Owner's Pay (salary) account
   *$300 would go into your Operating Expenses account

There are, of course, a lot of variables and nuances, and I highly recommend you read the book yourself to be able to really dive deep into it.

While your percentages may look a bit different, I'm going to use the above percentages to illustrate how to determine your budget for outsourcing.

DON'T FORGET ABOUT FIXED EXPENSES

Since you've already allocated money for Profit, Taxes and Owner's Pay, the money that you'll have to play with when it comes to outsourcing will come out of your Operating Expenses account.

Before you go out and blow all the money in your Operating Expenses account, first consider your ongoing monthly expenses. For example, at bare minimum you likely have web hosting fees, and an email service such as AWeber [Ref 7] or GetResponse [Ref 8]. If you haven't been keeping up with your bookkeeping and you're not sure what your regular expenses are, simply take a look at your credit card statement, and if you use one, your PayPal account. You may find that you have some expenses that you've forgotten about.

Once you've made note of those things, look at what you have left in your Operating Expenses account. That should give you a basic idea of what you can afford to spend on outsourcing.

One thing I love about the Profit First methodology is that especially once it's in place, it's easy to take a look at the balance in your Operating Expenses account and know whether or not you can afford to hire help.

It's definitely easiest to know whether or not you can afford a one-off expense compared to hiring a regular team member that you'll pay on retainer.

That brings us to the next chapter where we'll take a look at hiring temporary, part-time, or full-time team members.

Rebecca Livermore

Chapter 9

PART TIME, TEMPORARY OR FULL TIME

SOME GREAT NEWS FOR BLOGGERS and other entrepreneurs is that it's no longer necessary to hire employees, and it's definitely not required to hire full-timers.

In this chapter, we'll look at the pros and cons of hiring part-time, temporary and full-time team members.

HIRING TEMPORARY WORKERS

Hiring temporary workers is where many bloggers start. It's actually where I started, and if you haven't yet hired team members for your blog, this is where I recommend you start as well.

Temporary workers are often hired for one-off projects. For example, you may hire a web designer to set up your blog, or a graphic designer to create your logo. Or you may hire an agency to help you launch your blog, and once the launch is over, they no longer work for you.

Temporary workers are an excellent way to get your feet wet when it comes to hiring help.

When I first started hiring help, I loved hiring temporary workers because at the time I didn't feel super secure with my income, and I didn't know whether or not I could afford to hire someone on a regular basis.

In fact, I still prefer to hire short-term workers. There's something very freeing about hiring someone for a specific task, negotiating a fee, and not having any further obligation to keep paying them.

However, as much as I love the freedom of temporary workers, there is a downside. Since you have no long-term commitment to them, they also have no long-term commitment to you, and they may not be there the next time you need help.

For example, I hired a contractor in the Philippines to repurpose some of my blog content into PowerPoint slides so that I could put them on SlideShare [Ref 9]. Not only did she do a great job at a reasonable cost, she worked fast.

Unfortunately, at one point when I went to hire her for another gig, she was nowhere to be found. She wasn't to blame for this, as she had made no commitment to me, no doubt because I had made no commitment to her!

By all means, hire temporary workers, but just know that the perfect contractor you found may not be there when you need them most.

HIRING PART-TIME WORKERS

In most cases, the part-time workers you hire will also be independent contractors, but they have a higher-level of commitment than temporary workers.

It's important to note that when I say there is a higher level of commitment, I mean that they have a higher level of commitment to you AND you have a higher level of commitment to them.

While any worker can quit at any time, and while you can let any worker go at any time, from an ethical perspective, it's important to only hire a part-time worker when you can, in good conscience, commit to paying them a set amount on an ongoing basis.

One drawback to hiring part-time workers is that if they need full-time income, they will need to work for multiple clients in order to make ends meet. This means that while they may have a commitment to you, they also have a commitment to others, and since they can only do one thing at a time, your requests may sometimes take a back seat to the requests of their other clients.

If you do hire part-time workers, be sure to communicate ahead of time which things are priorities and any deadlines you may have for work that needs to be done.

For example, when I did podcast production work or blog writing for clients, there were set days for the publication of those posts. No matter how busy I was, and no matter the demands of other clients, I was obligated to meet those deadlines. However, there were other tasks that didn't have specific deadlines that sometimes had to wait due to my other obligations.

HIRING FULL-TIME WORKERS

To date, I myself have not hired full-time team members for my blog. I would say that most bloggers primarily hire temporary and part-time workers.

Having said that, as your blog grows, hiring full-time workers is something worth considering. The biggest perk is that a full-time worker may be more loyal to you, and at the very least shouldn't have the distraction that comes from working for other clients.

One thing to keep in mind is that hiring a full-time worker is a big commitment on your part. Not only will it be more costly, but I believe you have a moral obligation to go into the relationship only if you can afford to pay a full-time worker in the foreseeable future.

Rebecca Livermore

This doesn't mean that you would never need to lay off a team member. The financial situation of your blog may change. Or the direction you decide to go with your business may change and because of that, your needs may change as well.

But chances are, a full-time team member will be highly dependent on the income you provide, and may have perhaps even quit another job to work for you.

So, consider carefully the cost and the moral obligations before hiring full-time workers.

Getting Help for Free

IT'S BEEN SAID THAT THERE'S NO SUCH THING as a free lunch. I both agree, and disagree with that. Let me explain.

It IS possible to grow a team of people who help you with your blog, for free. However, in most cases, the relationships are reciprocal. You may, at times, be the one to get free help and at other times, you may be the one to give it.

In some cases, the giving and receiving may happen simultaneously, such as is the case with one of the options I cover in this section, Blogging Buddies.

While these free options cost in terms of time, I wanted to include them in this book for a couple of reasons. The first is that early on, you may not have the budget to hire people to work on your blog. The good news is that even if that's the case, that doesn't mean you have to do everything on your own.

In addition to that, even once you can afford to hire help, relationships are still important. We all need others who will walk alongside us, and share the journey with us. Likewise, we all have a lot of value to contribute to others, and we can do so for free, in certain types of relationships.

Rebecca Livermore

The purpose of this section is to help you think about free options for building your team. In it I'll cover:

*Mastermind Groups

*Blogging Buddies

*How you can use healthy competition to grow your blog

*And the importance of writers' (bloggers') groups

Chapter 10

MASTERMIND GROUPS

BEING PART OF A MASTERMIND can help you with many different aspects of your business, including your content creation.

Here are some ways that being part of a mastermind has helped me with my content.

ACCOUNTABILITY

As mentioned previously, my mastermind group keeps me accountable for the content I create.

The mastermind group that I'm in isn't specifically for content creation. However, we all share our goals for the coming week, and then report the next week on how we do. Not all, but many of my goals are related to content creation. Because of that, most weeks I report on how I did with my content creation goals that I set from the previous week.

Other times I share personal goals or goals related to other aspects of my business.

Now I'm not going to say that each week I give a glowing report to my group on how I did. But I will say that many times I'm working hard early in the morning on my mastermind days to finish up things that I said I would do before the next meeting.

FEEDBACK

My mastermind group gives me feedback on my content.

For me anyway, this isn't necessarily a weekly thing, but many times members in the group will share a link to a draft of a sales page, or some other type of content and then the other members in the group give suggestions for improvement. While we are all kind and supportive of each other, we are also very honest and give constructive criticism as appropriate.

HOW MY MASTERMIND GROUP WORKS

I want to share with you how the mastermind that I'm in works. This isn't to say that it is THE way to do a mastermind, but I'm hoping it will give you some ideas to help you get started, if you've never been part of one before, or if the one you're part of isn't working very well for you, here are some things you may want to keep in mind.

LIKE-MINDEDNESS

It helps to have like-minded people in your mastermind group.

In the case of my group, we are for the most part in different industries, but we were all part of a particular forum and because of that had a common perspective. That gave us a good foundation in terms of compatibility.

MEET CONSISTENTLY

We meet weekly, using Google Hangouts. This is free, and accommodates up to 10 participants. There isn't a recording option in private Google Hangouts, so we record using Camtasia or Screenflow so those who can't make the call can listen to the recording.

Do it Your Way

You don't have to meet weekly, and you don't have to do it online. That is just what works for us. You may want to, instead, meet only monthly, or as is the case with one of my friends, her mastermind meets only quarterly, but they meet in person and the meeting lasts for a couple of days.

A Place to Share Information Between Meetings

In addition to your meetings, have a place to share information.

When we first started, we used a private Google+ community [Ref 10]. Now we use Slack [Ref 11].

We also have a shared folder on Google Drive where we share information with each other. This enables us to communicate in a private place during the week, and also allows us to have a shared document library.

Rebecca Livermore

Chapter 11

BLOGGING BUDDIES

LONG AGO, I WORKED FOR A COMPANY where many writers wrote 10 or more articles per day. You didn't have to do that, but there was a large pool of article assignments to choose from, and as long as you were able to write fast, you could make decent money writing for this company. But it was hard, grueling work.

As you can imagine, writing 10 or more articles per day was no small task, especially when it needed to be done day in and day out. Many of these people had the added motivation of rent being due or other bills to pay and if they didn't get the articles written, they'd be in big trouble financially. And while such a driving need may seem like enough to get the job done, in many cases, a little extra push was needed. That extra push came in the form of "writing buddies."

DEEPER THAN TRADITIONAL ACCOUNTABILITY

Writing (or blogging) buddies are another form of accountability, but it goes a bit deeper than a traditional accountability relationship in that your blogging buddy works on a similar goal as you, and in most cases, works on the goal at the same time.

Because of this, it's important to have a writing buddy with a similar schedule, or a similar time block available for blogging. This isn't 100% required, but it is helpful because there's something significant and motivating about knowing that your blogging buddy is working at the very same time as you.

The good news is that your blogging buddy can be located in another city, state, or even country (as long as the scheduling works out) since you can connect virtually.

THERE'S MORE THAN ONE WAY TO SKIN A CAT

My father always said, "There's more than one way to skin a cat." What he meant by that was that there was more than one way to accomplish a goal. That's certainly the case when it comes to blogging buddies.

One is that you can find someone who wants to write during the same block of time each day as you. For instance, perhaps you've decided you want to write a blog post (or at least work on a longer blog post) at the same time each day.

Your blogging buddy would commit to writing at the same time, if at all possible. Ideally, you will check in with each other at the beginning and then again at the end of your blogging time. The check in doesn't have to be time consuming. It can be as simple as a text message saying something like, "starting now" and a text message at the end that stated how much you accomplished in your time.

For instance, you may text back that you completed a blog post, or that you got research done for a bigger piece of content, or that you wrote a certain number of words. Your writing buddy will, of course, do the same thing in return.

> If you have problems finding someone who can write during the same time block, while not ideal, you can write at any time during the day, and then at an agreed upon time, check in with each other to report on whether or not you accomplished your blogging goals.

Another option that is harder to organize is to have a small group of blogging buddies that sets aside a whole day periodically, such as once a month or quarter to have a blogging intensive day, where as many blog posts are written in the day as possible. For instance, if you meet monthly, you may have a goal of getting all of your blog posts for the month written by the end of the day. While this can also be done one-on-one, it's kind of fun to make an event out of it and do it with a small group of fellow bloggers.

Intensive blogging days require more focus and motivation than blogging during smaller blocks of time, and since these can have more of a "work party" feel to them, if you go this route, try having a few times a day when you check in as a group. For instance, you can get on Skype or a Google Hangout for a quick group chat for 15 minutes every two hours or so to check in and cheer each other on.

The bottom line is that we all need other people, and perhaps a blogging buddy is just what you need in order to turn your blogging dreams into reality.

Rebecca Livermore

Chapter 12

START A COMPETITION

IN ALL OF THE OTHER CHAPTERS IN THIS SECTION, while people are involved in every one of them, all of them are very individual focused, when it comes to specific goals.

As an example, in my mastermind group, we all report to each other on our goals for the coming week and then how we did, but we all have very different goals and are not in any way trying to "beat" each other. The same thing has been true with all of the relationships I've had with writing buddies. We are all focused on writing and reporting back to each other on the writing we're doing, but the goals of each person are unique, and there is no judgment regarding who gets the most done.

To a large degree, this is fine with me because by nature, I'm NOT a very competitive person. And yet competition can sometimes be very motivating when it comes to getting more blog posts written.

Here are a couple of ways to use competition to your advantage, when it comes to blogging productivity.

JOIN WITH LIKE-MINDED BLOGGERS

Find a group of like-minded bloggers who have a similar goal level. You don't want to compete with someone with way lower goals than you and you also don't want to compete with someone who has goals that are way higher than yours.

DETERMINE WHAT YOU'LL MEASURE

The easiest measurement, by far, is word count. Other things, such as the number of blog posts in a specified period of time aren't as good because you can have short blog posts that can be written in an hour, or long and super detailed posts that may take a full day or more of work. But the number of words is pretty straight forward.

DETERMINE THE LENGTH OF YOUR COMPETITION

Since competing is generally very strenuous, it's not the best option for a long-term approach. I would recommend a month. A month allows for each individual to have a life beyond the competition and gives those who may have a temporary setback a chance to regroup and catch up or perhaps even zoom ahead.

SET UP A PUBLIC REPORTING SYSTEM

Regular reporting on writing progress is a great way to keep everyone motivated! If you know that someone has just zoomed ahead of you, then you may skip watching that T.V. show that you really didn't need to see anyway, and instead, write.

You can have a private Facebook group where people report on how they're doing, but that can get kind of messy, since whoever posted last is bumped to the top, and you may have other types of posts going on also. It can be hard to keep track of what's going on inside of a private Facebook group. What I would recommend instead, is a private page on your WordPress blog that the participants can log into and check in. This can be easy to set up, and free.

SET UP A REWARD SYSTEM (OPTIONAL)

A reward system is a great way to add some extra motivation and even fun to your competition.

This doesn't have to be anything extravagant, but it can be a fun thing to do. For instance, if you are doing this with a group of local bloggers, the "losers" can take the winner out to dinner. If you are doing it long distance, each participant can kick in $10 or $25 to participate, and the winner takes all. Whatever you do, keep it fun and simple!

Rebecca Livermore

Chapter 13

JOIN A WRITERS' (BLOGGERS') GROUP

Writers' groups have been around for a long time, for good reason. Since writing is a solitary endeavor, it helps to get together with others (either online or in person) who have similar goals and who understand what goes into being a blogger. This can be similar to a mastermind group, but the focus is a bit different.

Here are some ideas for how to make the most of a bloggers' group

1. Make sure the focus of the particular group is on blogging, since many writers' groups focus on other types of writing such as articles or books.

2. Share each other's content. This shouldn't be a requirement, but it can be very helpful. It gets a bit sticky if people blog on topics you're not interested in or disagree with, or that your audience wouldn't find helpful. But when possible, sharing and commenting on each other's blog posts is something to consider.

3. Have "write ins." Get together, either in person or online, share some writing prompts, and then set a timer and see how much writing you can get done in that time.

4. Provide blog critiques. Take turns critiquing each other's blogs. The critiques should happen on a voluntary basis, and should be done in a positive but honest manner.

5. Provide blog post critiques. This is similar to blog critiques, but dig deeper and critique the actual blog posts, rather than the blog as a whole.

6. Write guest posts for each other's blogs This works best if people in your group write on topics that fit with the blog where they want to guest post.

7. Encourage each other. Early on in my days as a writer, I attended ONE meeting at a writers' group. Why? The people in the group were overly snooty, and ripped the writing that people shared to shreds. The last thing I wanted to do was to share anything I wrote in that group, so I never went back.

Obviously, solid critiques can be an important part of a blogging group, but make sure the overall tone of the group is encouraging and helpful.

8. Decide whether or not to have open or closed membership. I recommend closed, so that the relationships in the group can mature, and so that everyone in the group understands what the individual members are trying to accomplish with their blogs.

9. Include some type of instructional element. This is optional, but if people in the group have different areas of expertise, they can train other bloggers in the group in those areas.

10. Read and discuss a blogging or content marketing related book. Book discussions can be a great way to grow together as bloggers.

Hiring Your First Paid Team Members

ADDING FREE TEAM MEMBERS TO YOUR MIX is a great idea, but at some point – hopefully sooner rather than later – you'll need to pay people.

If the thought of that scares you, bear in mind what I wrote in the Introduction hat a little dab will do ya. Also refer to the information in Chapter 8 on setting a budget, and the information in Chapter 9 about hiring temporary and part-time help. In this section, I'll give you options for hiring help that start at $5.00

The bottom line is that hiring help doesn't have to break the bank.

Phew! Now that we have that out of the way, and you can relax a bit, let's take a look at what I'll cover in this section:

   *U.S. vs. Overseas

   *Where to Find Help [U.S. Based]

   *Where to Find Help [Philippines Based]

   *Where to Find Help [Personal Recommendations]

   *Using an Agency vs. Hiring Independent Workers

Rebecca Livermore
>*Temporary vs. Long Term Considerations

>*and Pros and Cons of Hiring Family Members

Let's go ahead and dive in.

Chapter 14

U.S vs. Overseas

WHENEVER THE TOPIC OF OUTSOURCING IS DISCUSSED, the issue comes up of whether or not to hire workers in the U.S. (or wherever you're located) or if you should hire team members in countries where the cost of living, and thus the wages are lower, such as the Philippines.

I've done both, and will likely continue to do both. The reason for that is simple: there are pros and cons to both options. That's what we'll take a look at in this chapter.

Pros and Cons of Hiring Overseas

Many bloggers choose to hire help from countries such as the Philippines. That can be a really great option, for a couple of reasons, with the most often cited reason being price.

No doubt about it, price is a huge consideration, especially in the beginning when your blog and business aren't making a ton of cash. But it's only one consideration.

Something that could be considered an advantage or a disadvantage is the time difference. Essentially, days and nights are the opposite. This works well if you like to assign tasks during the day and wake up the next morning to find them done.

However, if you like sending an email and getting a quick response, this may not be the best option for you. (Some overseas workers work the graveyard shift to compensate for the time difference, but it's not something I would personally ask someone to do, unless it fit with their other life priorities.)

For me a bigger issue is adapting to cultural differences. You can't hire someone from a different country and expect them to think like you do, and to work in the same way that someone from your own country would.

This doesn't mean that it won't work, but that you may need to educate yourself about the proper way to interact.

Cultural differences may also make it more challenging to use a VA from the Philippines in a more public role. This varies, person by person, and the one you hire may "sound like" someone from the U.S.

True story time: I once worked with an _excellent_ transcriber from the Philippines. Generally speaking, the work was good, but I noticed that sometimes things that would easily be caught by an American were mis-transcribed by this person. For example, when a reference was made to the energy drink, "Red Bull," it was transcribed as red ball.

Here's another humorous example: "being distracted by email pinging on the desktop" was transcribed as, "being distracted by a mule peeing on the desk top." That would indeed be distracting, now wouldn't it? Thankfully, I proofread and edited the transcript before it went live.

Now the truth of the matter is that even U.S. based transcribers will sometimes mishear what is said. But the cultural misunderstandings can lead to some interesting reading.

PROS AND CONS OF HIRING IN THE U.S.

The biggest con to hiring help in the U.S. is of course cost. Whereas you can hire full time help in the Philippines for as low as $500 per month (more or less, depending on the job) [Ref 13], even a minimum wage worker in the U.S. makes approximately $1350 per month. And naturally, you can't expect a highly-skilled person in the U.S. to work for minimum wage.

Another con to consider is that due to cost, you may be able to hire a full-time worker from the Philippines, but may not be able to afford to do so if you choose to hire someone in the U.S. [Refer back to Chapter 9 for the pros and cons of hiring full-time workers.]

Now on the plus side, team members that you hire in the U.S. "speak your language," both literally and figuratively. (English is also widely spoken in the Philippines, but the figurative aspect of it may be missing due to cultural issues.)

Being in the same or similar time zones can also be helpful especially when it comes to impromptu meetings, and real-time communication via email, Slack, etc..

LOCAL VS. NATIONAL

If you do decide to go with U.S. based team members, another decision to make is whether or not you want your team members to be local, or if they can live in any state.

In most cases, a desire for local team members stems from habit and sticking with what is comfortable, more than necessity. With the technology that we have available today, it's easy to share files in the cloud, chat via video, and do most everything from a distance.

One advantage to consider when it comes to hiring nationally vs. locally is that if you broaden your scope to national, you have a larger talent pool to choose from. It may make the hiring process a bit more challenging, but may also increase the odds of finding the perfect fit.

Rebecca Livermore

Having said that, if you have a lot of hands on projects that you'd like to do in person with team members or if you simply like a lot of face time, then hiring local may be right for you.

Rebecca Livermore

Chapter 15

AGENCY VS. INDEPENDENT

PERHAPS BY NOW YOU'VE MADE THE DECISION to hire U.S. based team members, or maybe you think that you're better off hiring people overseas. You may even, like me, want to do a combination of the two.

Once you've made that decision, the next thing you have to figure out is whether or not to go through an agency or to hire team members directly.

In this chapter, I'll provide you with some food for thought on which option may be best for you.

AGENCY ADVANTAGES

As is true with most, if not all things, there are pros and cons to hiring help through an agency.

Here are the top advantages:

#1: Pre-screening and Training

Agencies take the first steps when it comes to vetting potential candidates. They may do background checks, interviews, and perhaps even do some training.

As part of the screening process, they often also act as matchmakers, looking through their talent pool for team members that appear to be a good fit for you.

That can save you a lot of time and frustration, since much of the work is done ahead of time for you.

#2: Multiple Team Members

Some, but not all agencies assign more than one team member to you. One may be your primary worker, and the second one may be a backup, trained in all your basic tasks. This can really come in handy if your team member quits, becomes ill or has some other type of emergency that results in a quick exit.

#3: Deal with Hiring and Firing

Many years ago, I worked for a temp agency in the U.S. While on the surface it may have looked like I worked for one company, the reality is that a different company cut my paycheck, and dealt with issues. Thankfully I never really had a problem with this, but if the company that I worked for via the agency decided they wanted to get rid of me, they wouldn't even have to tell me – they would have simply communicated that to the agency, and the agency would have been the bearer of bad news.

While I'd prefer direct communication with team members, if a situation is particularly unpleasant, it can be nice to have an agency as the mediator.

AGENCY DISADVANTAGES

The advantages mentioned above are nothing to sneeze at, but no surprise, there are also some disadvantages. Here are three to consider:

#1: Potentially Higher Cost

As should come as no surprise, agencies often take a cut of what you pay for your workers. This is totally fair and appropriate, as they are providing a service to both you and to the team members.

An unfortunate disadvantage to this is that there is the potential for a higher price to you, and a lower amount of payment to the contractor.

If at some point, you decide to work directly with the VA, you may have to buy out the VA by paying a fee to the agency to work directly with the VA.

#2: May Not Get a Self-Starter

This next thing is a broad enough generalization that I almost didn't include it, but I think it's worth at least considering.

While not true in all cases, virtual workers who work for an agency may do so because they either don't have the drive or the know-how to drum up business on their own. They may have more of an employee mentality, as opposed to the mindset of a business owner.

Now perhaps that's a good thing if what you want is someone with an employee mindset. However, if you want a more independent thinker who knows how to make decisions on her own, comes up with innovative ideas, and is very driven, an independent person may be a better option, since those skills are needed for someone who runs their own business.

#3: Limited to Working with Their Talent Pool

If you decide to go with an agency, you'll be limited to the workers they have available. Some agencies are huge, and have a lot to choose from, and others may only have one or two options for you. If you choose not to limit yourself to working with an agency, you may have more freedom – and choices – about who you'll hire.

Rebecca Livermore
Independent Advantages and Disadvantages

In some ways, to understand the advantages and disadvantages to hiring help for your blog directly rather than through an agency, all you have to do is consider the opposite of the advantages and disadvantages of hiring help through an agency.

For example, when you hire a true independent contractor who represents him or herself, all of the money goes to the contractor, rather than some of it going to the agency and the remainder going to the contractor.

You will also have more freedom and flexibility in who you decide to hire, and you can negotiate the terms with greater freedom than you may be able to through an agency. You also won't have to jump through any hoops to work with the independent contractor directly, since that's what you did right from the start.

Those are all positives. But of course, hiring someone who works independently isn't all sunshine and roses.

Among other things, it may be harder and take more work to find the right person. For example, when Michael Hyatt decided to hire a podcast producer, he put an announcement on his blog about the job, which included a job description and instructions on how to apply. He received at least 100 applications, and it was up to this team to vet all of the applicants, narrow it down to a handful of candidates, and handle all of the interviews, salary negotiations, and so on. Ultimately it worked well for him as a few years later, the person they hired is still working in that capacity.

However, if the person hadn't worked out, he would have had to deal with firing him. In contrast, if he had gone through an agency, not only would the agency had done the hard work of finding the right person, they also could act as an intermediary if there were problems.

Rebecca Livermore

Chapter 16

WHERE TO FIND HELP [U.S. BASED]

IF YOU'VE DECIDED TO HIRE U.S. BASED HELP, there are many, many options to choose from. I'm going to provide just three companies as a starting place for you.

PRIORITY VA

Priority VA [Ref 14] is owned by my good friend, Trivinia Barber. I recommend her agency above many other U.S. based agencies in large part because Trivinia and I have both worked together, when we worked for two of the same clients (Michael Hyatt and Amy Porterfield). When you work with someone directly over a long period of time, you learn of their integrity level, their proficiency level, and how they handle pressure. Trivinia does a great job on all fronts.

Trivinia and I were teammates when she started Priority VA, and I saw firsthand her diligence in finding not just good team members, but great ones. Her team is small enough to have a small family feel, and large enough to have a good talent pool, with a lot of different service offerings that range from general VA work such as email management and scheduling, to content writing, podcast production, graphic design, WordPress and more.

Fancy Hands

Fancy Hands [Ref 15] is a great way to take a baby step into hiring help. If you have a very limited budget and don't know if you have enough work for hiring even a part-time team member, Fancy Hands is worth a try.

The basic concept of Fancy Hands is that you pay a monthly fee that at the time of this writing ranges from $29.99 per month for five tasks, all the way up to $399.99 per month for unlimited tasks. Naturally, the bigger the commitment, the lower the cost per task.

The catch with Fancy hands is that each task should take 15 minutes or less. If you have a bigger project, then you will need to pay for multiple tasks to get the project done. In addition to that, you won't have a dedicated VA. Between those two things, you can't expect to assign complex tasks to Fancy Hands. However, it's a great way to start with outsourcing, particularly if your budget is super tight.

I personally think that the best course of action is to hire more permanent team members, and use Fancy Hands for smaller tasks you don't want to bother your other team members with.

WPCurve

If as a blogger you've ever messed up your website, or perhaps wanted to change something on it and couldn't quite figure out how to do so, WPCurve [Ref 16] may be just the thing you need.

The current pricing starts at $79 per month, and includes unlimited 30-minute WordPress tasks. The basic way it works is that you submit a small task, and as soon as they complete that task, you can submit another one. If you have a bigger task, you'll need to break it into smaller ones.

WPCurve is an affordable way to get professional help for your WordPress site.

Rebecca Livermore

Chapter 17

WHERE TO FIND HELP [PHILIPPINES BASED]

THE PHILIPPINES HAS BECOME THE place to hire team members at an affordable cost. There are other low-cost countries where you can find help as well, but the Philippines comes out ahead of many of the others, for a couple of reasons, with one of the main ones being that English is widely spoken.

The options below are a great place to start if you want to hire workers in the Philippines.

VIRTUAL STAFF FINDER

Virtual Staff Finder (VSF) [Ref 17] is the best know and the best run site for finding virtual workers from the Philippines. It's best for hiring permanent part-time or full-time assistants. While the term VA is used, they can help you find more than just general virtual assistants. At the time of this writing, they offer help finding the following types of virtual workers:

*General virtual assistants

*SEO specialists

*WordPress developers

Rebecca Livermore
*Graphic designers

Below is the basic process for working with Virtual Staff Finder

SIGN UP FOR THE SERVICE

This is the step to take once you've decided you're serious about hiring a permanent part-time or full-time virtual assistant from the Philippines. At the current time, there is a one-time sign up cost of $495. Once you pay that fee, the Virtual Staff Finder team will send you a sample job description. You'll use that to list what you need your VA to do.

Prepare for Your New Assistant

After you sign up, you'll have access to training videos that have been created by Chris Ducker. In the videos, he provides tips to help you get ready for your new VA.

Interview

Once they've found some potential candidates for you, they test them, do background checks, and conduct phone (and when possible) in-person interviews. By the end of this process, they'll narrow it down to the top three candidates for the position.

Hire

You can then interview the three candidates that VSF selected for you, and determine which one you want to hire.

The virtual workers you hire through VSF are employed by you, not VSF, so you pay the team members directly. You won't pay any ongoing costs to Virtual Staff Finder.

I myself have not used Virtual Staff Finder, but I personally know Chris Ducker, and he's top-notch. I also personally know many business owners who have hired assistants through VSF with good results.

ONLINEJOBS.PH

OnlineJobs.Ph [Ref 18] is a "no frills" option for hiring virtual staff from the Philippines.

Basically, the way that it works is that you can search their database of job seekers, for free. However, if you want to contact the worker, you have to pay a fee, which at the current time cost $49 per month.

The good news is that once you hire someone, you can drop that monthly commitment, if desired.

OnlineJobs.Ph is very different from Virtual Staff Finder in that you have to do all of the legwork when it comes to searching for suitable workers, reaching out to them, interviewing them, etc. Because of that, if you want a lot of help with the process of finding and vetting potential team members from the Philippines, Virtual Staff Finder is a better bet.

If you're concerned about knowing whether or not your newly hired worker is actually working, OnlineJobs.Ph has a time tracking feature. You can have your team member log in each time she works, so you have no doubt as to the amount of time that is spent on the job.

The time tracking option works even if you are no longer paying the monthly fee.

FIVERR

Fiverr [Ref 19] isn't specifically Philippines based, and in fact some of the people on Fiverr are in the U.S. In spite of that, I decided to put Fiverr under the Philippines section because due to the low cost, many of the people you'll hire through Fiverr are located in countries with a lower cost of living, such as the Philippines.

As the name implies, Fiverr tasks cost $5. Before you get too excited, let me say that my experience with Fiverr is that it's a bit hit or miss.

You may have to hire multiple people to get the desired outcome. Even so, at only $5 a pop, you don't have a lot to lose.

Another problem that I've had with Fiverr is that some of the best people disappear over time. Some use Fiverr as a way to get their name out there, and then quit once they have all the business they need outside of Fiverr.

Popular providers also are under high demand, and because of it may have a slow turnaround time for projects.

Fiverr contractors provide a wide variety of tasks that run the gamut including everything from transcription to proofreading or editing, to creating blog graphics and more.

People who use Fiverr can rate and review the services they purchased, so take the time to read some of the ratings and reviews before making a decision on who to hire.

I wouldn't consider Fiverr to be a great place for ongoing work, but it's a good way to get small tasks done at a very reasonable price.

Chapter 18

How to Find Independent Workers

If you decide that you'd prefer to hire team members that are independent rather than hiring ones that work for an agency, the best way to go about that is through personal recommendations.

Ask other people in your industry or who perhaps have team members that do tasks similar to what you'll need who they know. You can also ask your general network for leads.

Write a Job Description

Before you reach out to your network for leads, write a job description that lays out the skills and requirements for the position.

This will help your friends and colleagues to have a better idea of your needs. It also provides them with something they can pass on to potential candidates.

Advertise through Your Own Network

Once you've written up your job description, post it on your blog.

You can link to the blog post and share it on social media, including any groups that allow that type of posting. For example, you may be in a

Rebecca Livermore

Facebook group with other business owners. Some of those people may be potential team members, or may know of qualified candidates. Just be sure to follow the guidelines of the specific groups before you link to your post.

Rebecca Livermore

Chapter 19

ALL IN THE FAMILY

MANY BLOGGERS I KNOW HIRE FAMILY MEMBERS to assist with their blog. I myself have done the same thing.

My daughter has worked as my VA, doing a lot of general admin tasks for me such as research and transcription.

My husband provides editing help, formatting, and other content related tasks.

And my son has provided help with graphic design.

Through my own experience and through the stories that other bloggers have shared with me about hiring family members, I've learned that there are both pros and cons to hiring family members to assist you with your blog.

BENEFITS OF HIRING FAMILY MEMBERS

First, let me go over the benefits.

High Trust Level

I've heard horror stories of untrustworthy family members who steal and otherwise abuse family relationships. You know better than anyone whether or not your family members would be so inclined.

In my experience, the trust level that I have with my family members is very high. I've enjoyed having them work for me because I feel comfortable providing them with full access to my bank accounts and other sensitive accounts in a way that I may not with others.

Have a Vested Interest in the Business

If your blog and business are a success, your family members directly benefit. Because of that, and because of the fact that they love you, they have a different level of interest in the success of your business than the average team member.

May be Cheaper

Your family members may be cheaper labor than other team members you hire. This is primarily true if they are younger, and still living at home.

Good if You're Going to Pay Them Anyway

If you're like most parents, and if your teens and college-aged "kids" are like most, they need money from you on a regular basis. You can just hand them money, or you can ask them to work for it.

Personally, I think that having them work for it is a better option, so long as they have the right skill set that fits with what you need.

Working for money not only helps you out (since you get something in exchange for the money you give), but it also provides a higher sense of self-worth for your family members if they earn the money you provide for them.

In addition to that, as long as the family members are working for the pay they receive, you can write what you pay them off on your taxes, which of course you can't do if you simply hand money to them. (Be sure to consult with your tax professional for details. For online business, I recommend The Bottom Line.)

DISADVANTAGES OF HIRING FAMILY MEMBERS

As much as I enjoy having my family members assist me with my blog, it doesn't always work out for everyone. Here are a few disadvantages to hiring family members.

May Not Take Work Seriously

Your family members may not take work as seriously as people you hire who aren't related to you. After all, the work they do is just for "Mom" (or whatever relationship you are to them). Because of that, they may not view you as a real boss or the job as a real job.

Harder to Fire

Family members are definitely harder to fire simply because of the dynamics in the relationship. If you fire another team member, you may never see them again. In fact, you may have never met them at all in person. In contrast, if you fire a family member, you will likely see them on a regular basis, even after things fall apart.

In addition to that, you may be more reluctant to fire them since you're more aware of their personal financial situation, and more invested in their well-being and happiness.

Other Team Members May Resent

If you have a mix of team members that are related to you as well as ones that are not, the non-family members may resent the family members who work for you.

To avoid this type of team conflict, it's important to have the same standards, including the same pay structure for everyone. For example, if you have a family member and also a non-family member do the same tasks, you should pay them the same amount.

You also need to make sure that you treat everyone the same. For example, it's not fair if you have required team meetings and the only person who routinely misses the team meeting is related to you.

If you feel like you can't be objective in working with family members, it may be best if you avoid hiring people who are related to you.

Outsourcing Ideas to Get You Started

HOPEFULLY BY NOW YOU'RE CONVINCED that outsourcing is a good idea. You may have started off by building your "free" dream team and have perhaps made the decision whether or not to hire assistants in your home country, or perhaps you've decided to outsource overseas. Or maybe like me, you've decided to do a combination of the two.

Regardless of the choices you've made, congratulations for getting to this point!

Now the work of figuring out what tasks to outsource can begin in earnest. That's what this section is all about.

Rebecca Livermore

Chapter 20

GENERAL VA

A GENERAL VA FITS INTO WHAT MANY PEOPLE would consider to be a basic administrative assistant. The General VA you hire may not even have blog-related experience, but should still be a great asset in the areas similar to the ones listed below.

EMAIL MANAGEMENT

If your blog is at a point where you get a lot of email, then having someone else handle your email for you can be a big help. You can have the same assistant handle your blog-related email, as well as other aspects of your business email.

Generally speaking, I recommend having the assistant reply to people as herself, rather than pretending to be you. Create email templates that can be used to respond to the common types of email you receive.

SCHEDULE INTERVIEWS

As your blog and business grows, you'll likely be asked to make guest appearances on podcasts. Instead of taking the time yourself to go back and forth with someone arranging the time, let your assistant do it for you.

NETWORK WITH REVENUE SOURCES

Let your assistant, in a sense, cover her own salary by finding revenue opportunities for you and your blog. For example, she may be able to arrange for sponsorships for your podcast, or find affiliate programs that fit with your blog and brand. Have her reach out, make all the connections, set up affiliate accounts and so on.

MANAGE YOUR AFFILIATE PROGRAM. . .

Speaking of affiliate accounts, your VA can manage your own affiliate program and interact with affiliates for your products and programs on your behalf. She can also keep up with the bookkeeping on what is owed to each affiliate.

TRANSCRIBE AUDIO

If you have a podcast or do webinars, transcripts are a great value add for your followers. Many virtual assistants have mad typing skills and can handle transcription without a problem.

If you prefer to speak than write, but still want written blog posts, create an outline, dictate your thoughts, and have your assistant transcribe it. With a bit of clean up, it's an easy way to get a blog post written, without any actual writing.

RESEARCH GUEST POST OPPORTUNITIES

Want to expand your reach by guest posting on other blogs? Let your assistant do the leg work on finding opportunities for you. He can also reach out to bloggers to arrange opportunities for you, keep a spreadsheet with contact information of the blogs and places your posts have been published, and so on.

If desired, he can also find people to guest post on your blog, and manage that process for you. Alternatively, you can assign that task to your content manager, as you'll see in the next chapter.

Chapter 21

CONTENT MANAGER

NOWADAYS, A LOT OF PEOPLE HIRE A VIRTUAL ASSISTANT, for good reason! VAs can be a great addition to your team. And while a "general" VA can help you with handling email, scheduling, and many other duties as mentioned in the previous chapter, a content manager, or what some would refer to as a blog assistant is someone who specializes specifically in blog-related duties.

For example, your content manager can upload your blog posts, format them, add in SEO meta data, proofread, find and add images to your post, and even promote your blog posts on social media. The bottom line is that a content manager can make your blog better and save you a ton of time.

Here are some other things you may want your content manager to do:

*Manage comments. Have him respond to comments as himself, introducing himself as a member of your team. He can also delete any spammy or inappropriate comments.

*Block trouble makers. Unfortunately, as your blog grows, so may the trouble makers. Your content manager can block repeat offenders.

*Maintain your editorial calendar. An editorial calendar will increase the odds that you'll always have a fresh supply of content on your blog. In addition to that, if your content is planned ahead of time, there's a greater chance that it will help you meet your objectives. But editorial calendars take time to manage, so why not assign the task to your content manager?

*Coordinate guest bloggers. This task can be done through a partnership between your virtual assistant and your content manager, or be handled exclusively by your content manager. This task can include making sure posts are received on time, are edited properly, and uploaded and formatted.

Now notice that none of these steal your voice. The content manager isn't writing your content. He or she is simply taking what you've created and doing a lot of the behind the scenes work on the content. If you're a busy blogger, and if you have the budget to hire help, this is a great way to spend some of that money. (Side note: your content manager can also play the role of helping you with research, as outlined in Chapter 23.)

*Writing, editing and proofreading. As I mentioned in Chapter 5, the one thing you shouldn't outsource is the actual writing. I do make an exception for that in that the writing can be done by someone else if it's based on your other content. For example, your content manager can write the show notes for your podcast, since they're based on the audio that you created. Blogging Your Voice (explained in the next chapter), is also an option.

You can also use your content manager to edit and proofread your writing, slide presentations and other content.

Chapter 22

BLOGGING YOUR VOICE

IF YOU WANT TO INCLUDE WRITTEN CONTENT on your blog, but don't want to do any actual writing yourself, one thing you might want to consider is allowing someone such as your content manager or another writer to "blog your voice." In the past, I provided this service for clients and in fact have written hundreds of blog posts for people who prefer not to do any writing themselves, but who see the value of written content.

Here's how it works:

*Plan out the blog posts you want to have written for the next month. Come up with the title, and the main points.

*Connect with your writer via Skype or some other conference call option with recording capabilities.

*Have your writer "interview" you about each of the blog posts. For example, they may start off by saying just the title of the post. That will be your cue to start talking about the points in the post.

*While you're talking, the writer should listen for things that aren't clear. He may also make note of other things that could make the post more interesting, such as stories or illustrations.

*Once you finish your "spiel," have the writer ask you to tell stories that illustrate the point, explain any terms you used that may not be clear to your readers, and so on.

*After the interview is complete, the writer can have the interview transcribed, and use the transcript as the basis for the blog post. Note that the editing that the writer does should go far beyond cleaning up the transcript. The goal is for the writer to turn your ramblings into a solidly written blog post while keeping your actual words intact as much as possible.

Since your actual words are used to a large degree, this method makes it possible to retain your voice even if you don't do any of the actual writing.

Chapter 23

RESEARCH ASSISTANT

RESEARCH IS ONE OF THE BEHIND THE SCENES aspects of blogging that can definitely be outsourced. This is true because the research that is done doesn't impact the voice in which the material is presented. Research is the raw material that you, the blogger, will turn into content for your blog.

I won't go as far as to say that anyone can do the research for you, because knowing how to research is in and of itself a skill that some people have and some don't. Here's an analogy that comes to mind:

If you were a dressmaker, you could outsource finding the raw materials -- the fabric, trim, buttons, and so on, to someone else. You could then turn that into a beautiful dress. But if the person you outsourced this task to didn't have an eye for design, and chose low quality fabric and accessories, or things that just didn't go well together, in spite of how skillful of a seamstress you are, the end product wouldn't be great.

I bring this up because when you do outsource, whether that be research or anything else, you need to be sure to select someone with the right skill set, who will approach the project with the same level of care that you would if you were doing it yourself. Because of this, cheaper isn't always better.

Rebecca Livermore

Now, having said that, here are some of the types of things you can have a research assistant do for you.

IDEA GENERATION

Start by having your research assistant come up with a certain number of ideas for your blog. For example, you may ask her to come up with 20 blog post ideas for each of the categories on your blog. I recommend asking for twice as many ideas as you need, since you may not like all of them.

Have her come up with ideas by doing keyword research, checking to see what types of things come up when doing Google searches, searches on YouTube, digging up what other bloggers in your niche are blogging on, and so on.

FIND RESOURCES

Once she generates ideas for your blog, select the ones you want to use. Then have her find resource material for each of those posts. For instance, you may have her find you 10 different articles that pertain to each blog post title.

Have him or her add all of those ideas to Evernote or OneNote.

(Side note: one great thing about using something like the Evernote or OneNote Web Clippers is that the original article will be linked to so you can properly cite your sources. It's important to give credit where credit is due!)

ORGANIZE INFORMATION

Your research assistant can then take the information gleaned, and create a document for you, with chunks of the research put under each point on the document. For instance, let's say that you were to write a post about the best tires to buy for an SUV. Your research assistant would perhaps find information on the different types of SUV tires, different companies that make tires, consumer reports, cost, and so on.

Relevant pieces of information could be copied and pasted from Evernote into a Google Doc, under the right subhead. This is an important step because there may be only one relevant paragraph in an entire article, and rather than having to read all of the articles and organize the information yourself, your research assistant could do that for you. In this document, make sure they link to the original source of the information.

There are likely many other ways you can have someone else do research for you. The next time you do research for an article, jot down the steps you take to do research, and the types of things you may be able to hire someone else to do for you.

Rebecca Livermore

Chapter 24

SOCIAL MEDIA MANAGER

IN THE SAME WAY THAT I BELIEVE that as a blogger you should create your own content, I also believe you should be the primary one interacting with people on social media. After all, you are the name and face associated with your blog and brand.

At the same time, that doesn't mean that you need to do everything yourself. Here are a few ways that a social media manager can help.

SOURCE CONTENT

Have your social media manager find content for you to share on your social media channels. One of the best ways to do this is to create a list of bloggers whose content you like and want to share with your fans. You can organize that information on Twitter lists [Ref 22] or in "subscribe to blogs" on Feedly [Ref 23]. Once you've set that up, be sure to communicate the types of content you want to share. For instance, let your social media manager know if you prefer to avoid sharing content that is promotional in nature.

MONITOR CONVERSATIONS

Nowadays one of the first things disgruntled people do is turn to social media. This is especially true if they purchase a product and aren't happy. If they don't get a quick response from your team after reaching out via email or through a contact form, they may voice their frustration about the experience on social media.

The last thing you want to do is let a long time go by before responding to a complaint like that. While none of us like complaints and dislike them even more when they're done in public, public complaints that are responded to quickly and professionally can actually improve your image, rather than hurt it. But the response needs to happen quickly, the sooner the better. Since none of us spend all of our time on social media (or at least we shouldn't!), a social media manager that keeps tabs on the activity on your social media profiles can be a lifesaver.

CREATE CONTENT

Under your supervision, your social media manager can craft tweets, images, and other types of content for you. I do recommend keeping an eye out on what is being posted since it will be posted under your name.

POST CONTENT YOU'VE CREATED

Even if you create the content yourself, a social media manager can save you a ton of time by posting that content for you. They can either post it in real time or upload it to social media tools such as Edgar [Ref 24] or Buffer [Ref 25].

One thing to keep in mind is that while your content manager represents you by responding to comments and other interactions on your social media profiles, they should always sign their posts with their own name. For one thing, it's the honest thing to do. Just think of how your readers would feel if they thought you were interacting with them only to later find out that it was someone pretending to be you.

In addition to that, if by chance they say something you don't quite agree with, it's best if it's not done with your name.

HANDLE ADS

Advertising is one of the best ways to use social media platforms such as Facebook [Ref 26]. But it can be time-consuming to create and monitor ads. Stay involved in the plan for ads including input on the creation of the ads, budget and so on, but let your social media manager do the grunt work of getting the ads live and monitoring them while they run.

ONGOING EDUCATION

It can be hard to keep up with all the changes on the various social media platforms. Let your social media manager take care of that for you. One of the best ways to go about that is to purchase programs for him and pay him to take the time to go through them. You can even have him write summaries of the training he goes through on your dime.

A social media manager can increase the traffic to your blog and be a key player when it comes to building your online following.

Rebecca Livermore

Chapter 25

IMAGE CREATION

IMAGES FOR BLOG POSTS AND SOCIAL MEDIA are all the rage. In fact, a whole range of tools and training now exist for the purpose of creating blog and social media images. But image creation can be time consuming, and while with the tools now available "anyone" can create images, not everyone can do them well.

One thing to bear in mind is that true graphic designers can be expensive. They aren't always, but graphic design is indeed a highly specialized skill and it can also be time consuming. That's the bad news.

The good news is that with easy-to-use tools such as Canva [Ref 27], PicMonkey [Ref 28], and Pixlr [Ref 29], Photoshop knowledge is no longer a prerequisite for image creation. A creative person with an eye for color and a knack for design can use these tools and turn out decent images for your blog and social media. Since they aren't graphic designers in the truest sense of the word, their rates may be more affordable.

Rebecca Livermore

Chapter 26

HAVE YOUR BLOG REVIEWED

MOST OF THE TIME WHEN WE THINK ABOUT HIRING help for our blog, we think about hiring people to write, edit, upload, promote on social media, and so on. All of those are great ways to get help, but there is one other way that I'd like you to consider, and that is hiring someone to review your blog.

The interesting thing about this option is that instead of taking work off your plate, a blog review can actually add work to your plate -- at least temporarily.

For instance, a blog review may -- and actually SHOULD -- point out changes that you need to make on your blog. As an example, you may find that you need to, among other things, rewrite your "about" page. Doing so will require time, no doubt about it.

But blogging is about more than just cranking out blog posts; it's about building a business, and if your blog isn't maximized, then it won't be as effective as it could be. Because of that, while you may initially have work to do after having your blog reviewed, it can actually save you time in the long run if as a result of it, your blog performs better.

Here are some things to look for when it comes to hiring a blog reviewer.

Rebecca Livermore

1. The reviewer needs to have a successful blog. This is a tricky and somewhat subjective thing, because you can't necessarily tell if someone else's blog is effective. For instance, a blog may have a lot of comments, and yet not generate any income, and therefore (if income was an objective for the blog) the blog isn't successful. Or a blog may have only a few comments, and yet provide the owner with a full client load or good product sales, and therefore be successful.

Since it's impossible to know that about someone else's blog, I would judge it more on the professionalism of the blog.

2. You need to like the style of the blogger. This doesn't mean that their style needs to mirror yours, but rather that you like the overall vibe and personality of the blogger offering the reviews. The reason that this is important is because a blog review is a pretty personal thing, and it will help if you enjoy the style of the person doing the review.

3. The review needs to be delivered in a format that works for you. For example, I prefer video reviews, because I can stop and start the video again and again as I implement what is taught in the review. If the review is done "in person" (meaning online via Skype, etc.) I would still want the review to be recorded via video, so that I could replay it later. Your preferences may be different, but just be sure to think about whether or not the style fits with what you most need.

4. It shouldn't be too cheap. Most of us are price conscious, for good reason -- we don't have an unlimited amount of money to spend on our blogs. But as price conscious as I am, I would be wary of someone who did blog reviews for much under $100. Typical pricing for blog reviews done by a professional should run between $97 and $500, depending on the level of demand of the reviewer, their experience level, and also what is included in the review.

As an example, at least at the time of this writing, I'm not offering blog reviews, but when I did, I offered them at the $97 level, which is on the low end of what I recommend in terms of pricing. The reviews I did consisted of a 15-minute video that I delivered to the client. Of course, it took me more than 15 minutes since I first had to review the blog, make notes and so on before recording the video. But it was done on my own schedule, and didn't require any live time with the reviewee, so that was a price that worked for me. If I was going to offer the live phone call after the review as an option, the price would need to be quite a bit higher.

At any rate, getting feedback on your blog by a professional blogger is definitely a worthwhile thing to have done, as it can really help you to move forward with your blogging goals.

Rebecca Livermore

Training Your Team

PERHAPS YOU'VE MADE THE PLUNGE AND HIRED (or made the decision to hire) your first team member(s).

Congratulations!

The next step is training!

I recall one job in particular where I was given about five minutes of training and then left to figure everything out myself. From what I could tell, the company was happy with my work, but I never felt good about it because I always had this nagging feeling that I didn't really know what I was supposed to do. Perhaps you, too, have suffered on a job in this way.

Not only does a lack of training cause a lot of stress for team members, it also increases the odds that work won't be done in a satisfactory manner. After all, if you don't clearly communicate what you want done and how to do it, how can you expect team members to do things right?

Rebecca Livermore

Chapter 27

TRAINING TAKES TIME

ONE OF THE BIGGEST REASONS THAT BLOGGERS fail to train their team members properly is that training takes time. In fact, if you compare the time it takes to train someone versus doing something yourself, you may be tempted to give up on the whole team idea and keep doing everything on your own. Trust me, I've been there! But that's a shortsighted way of looking at it. In the long run, properly trained team members can save you both time, and money.

One way to keep from being overwhelmed with the training process is to hire just one new team member at a time, and train him on a single task. Once you get the kinks worked out in the training and things are humming along with that one task, you can add new tasks.

I like to start very small and simple, with a task that requires minimal training, so that my new team member can get started right away, with very little supervision. While that beginning task is worked on, I work on creating training for the next task I want to assign.

CREATE TRAINING BEFORE HIRING

In an ideal world, you should create training before you actually hire people. This doesn't mean that you have to have a massive training library built before you hire your first team member. But do consider

Rebecca Livermore

getting at least some basic training materials in place before your new hire starts. That can make things much less stressful (and much more productive) for everyone!

Rebecca Livermore

Chapter 28

CREATE PROCESSES

A PROCESS IS SIMPLY A SERIES OF STEPS you take to achieve a desired result. We all have processes in every aspect of our lives. For instance, most of us use the same process over and over again to make a pot of coffee. We do those steps without thinking about it day in and day out, and because the steps are the same each time, we can expect to start each day with a perfect cup of coffee.

Creating processes for your blog ensures that the desired outcome is accomplished each time. Processes should be detailed enough and easy to understand to the degree that anyone with the proper skillset can do the tasks simply by following the process.

It's important to have processes in place for every task that is done on a regular basis in your business and blog. This includes processes for YOU to follow as well.

If you create documented processes for yourself to follow, not only will the quality of your work be more consistent, if you decide to hand a particular task off to someone else, you'll already have everything in place, and the training time will be minimal.

WHAT TO INCLUDE IN PROCESSES

The key and most important thing to keep in mind is that a process should include a list of EVERY single step that needs to be done in order for the task to be completed properly.

I like to create a checklist for each task. The checklist should be in logical, sequential order. Ideally, the checklist should be clutter free, but link to documents and videos that explain each step-in detail.

For instance, the process for uploading a new blog post to WordPress may have starting a new post in WordPress as the first step While this is a very basic step for anyone familiar with WordPress, make no assumptions about what the person you assign the task to does or doesn't know. Assume they don't know how to do the specific step in the process. Create a screenshare video or written documentation that demonstrates how to do the step.

Including a link to the detailed documentation or tutorial video on the checklist keeps the checklist uncluttered, but provides additional instruction the team member can refer to if needed.

If you create this level of documentation in your procedure creation, a brand-new team member without experience in an area can do the tasks by simply following the steps you laid out and referring to the training documents and videos. You can even have another team member fill in for the person who normally does the task if the person is ill, on vacation, or stops working for you.

TOOLS TO USE IN PROCESS CREATION

It's best to provide documentation for your procedures in multiple forms, such as written documentation (that includes screengrabs when appropriate), checklists and videos.

Thankfully, most if not all of the tools needed to document your processes are free, and in many cases, may come preinstalled on your computer.

At the most basic level you need a word processing program, a way to take screenshots, and a program for making videos.

Word Processing

For word processing, I've used Microsoft Word, Google Docs and OneDrive. Both Google Docs and OneDrive are free. If you're a Mac user you may want to use Pages, but keep in mind that you'll need to save the documents in a format that both Mac and Windows users can work with.

Screenshots

Your computer may come with a screengrab tool already installed. For instance, Windows computers have the "Snipping Tool" and the "Print Screen" option as standard. The Print Screen option is good if you want to take a screengrab that shows what you've selected from a dropdown window, but otherwise, the Snipping Tool is usually a better option.

Both Mac and PC users can use the free service, Jing [Ref 30], for taking screenshots.

I also really like Snagit [Ref 31] for screenshots because it has more options for marking up my images than Jing does. Snagit and Jing are both made by Techsmith, and are available for both Mac and Windows computers. However, Snagit is not free. At the current time it runs about $50.

I recommend starting with Jing, and then if you want something more robust, purchasing Snagit.

Videos

The great news is that both Jing and Snagit can also be used to create screenshare videos.

You can also use Screenflow [Ref 32] (Mac only) or Camtasia [Ref 33] (available for both Mac and PCs), but most likely Jing or Snagit are all you'll need for training purposes.

SWEETPROCESS

As your team grows, you may want to invest in SweetProcess. SweetProcess [Ref 34] is a tool for documenting procedures. It allows you to create step-by-step procedures and add videos, screen grabs, and so on to the processes. Each process has a checklist that team members can use as they work through the process. It's pretty slick, and I definitely recommend it if you want to take your process creation and presentation to the next level.

HAVE TEAM MEMBERS CREATE PROCESSES

One of the best ways to create processes for everything is to have your team members create them for you. This can be done if you hire team members who have more experience than you in certain areas. You can also have team members update processes as things change, or if they have ideas for improving some of your processes.

In addition to that, you can create a process in one form, and have the team member create a detailed process from what you initially created. For instance, you might make a quick screencast video as you're doing a process. The team member could take that and from it create a written checklist, written documentation with screengrabs, and so on. You can even have them recreate a more polished version of the video if the video you created was done on the fly and not the best quality.

Chapter 29

USE TRAINING CREATED BY OTHERS

MANY PROGRAMS THAT YOU USE may already have excellent tutorials in place. If that's the case, there may be no need to reinvent the wheel. Simply create a written checklist and in the checklist link to the training videos and documents that already exist.

You may also find great tutorials by independent users on YouTube.

The upside of doing this is that you don't have to take the time to create the training materials yourself. The downside is that you have no control over those videos since someone else owns the content. They could be deleted at any time. In addition to that, you may have specific ways you want things done that don't exactly fit with the videos created by others.

In spite of the drawbacks, the bottom line is that using training videos and written documents created by others can save you a lot of time.

I've also found excellent training programs on Lynda [Ref 35] and Udemy [Ref 36].

Rebecca Livermore

How to Securely Share Your Files and Passwords

ONCE YOU'VE HIRED TEAM MEMBERS, you'll need to share files and passwords with them. At the most basic level, you can forward emails with attachments to share documents, and you can share passwords via email or over the phone.

While using a very basic approach like that may work, it's not the most efficient way to go about it. The good news is, using the tools covered in this section will make managing your team easier and more efficient.

Rebecca Livermore

Chapter 30

TOOLS FOR SHARING PASSWORDS AND FILES

IN THIS CHAPTER, I'M GOING TO SHARE six tools you can use to share files and passwords. I've used all of them with great results. The best thing is that they all are free, or have free options available, so even if you're on a tight budget, they'll work for you.

All of the options are cloud based, so you can access them from any computer, and share them with your teammates without emailing documents back and forth.

GOOGLE DRIVE

Google Docs was the first tool that I used for collaborating with team members. I've used it with my own team members and my clients have also used it to collaborate with me on projects.

Google Drive [Ref 37] consists of several programs. The most popular ones are:

*Google Docs (similar to Microsoft Word)

*and Google Sheets (similar to Excel).

You can also use it to create forms which can be used for surveys, and slide presentations that are similar to PowerPoint.

Rebecca Livermore

In addition to that, you can use it for file storage and upload videos, images, .PDF files, .mp3 files, etc.

Many people find Google Drive to be a great file sharing option and all they need for sharing documents with team members. It's an especially good option if you already use other Google products such as gmail and Google calendar.

One drawback to Google Drive is that the products are essentially Microsoft knockoffs. If you're used to working with programs such as Microsoft Word and Excel, you may be frustrated by the lack of some of the features you're used to using if you switch to Google.

The good news is that you can create documents in other programs such as Word and upload them to Google Drive and from there share them with your team members. You can also download documents you created in Google Drive and work on them using your desktop applications.

In Google Drive you can share files with others and assign different permission levels to each user. For instance, you may allow some team members to only view documents, and others to edit them.

One huge plus to using Google Drive is that it's very popular, and because of that will likely integrate with many of the other programs you use.

ONEDRIVE

OneDrive [Ref 38] is very similar to Google Drive. In fact, it has the same basic features found in Google Drive. The biggest difference is that it is owned by Microsoft and because of that, rather than having knock off programs, it has "real" Microsoft Word, Excel, PowerPoint, and so on.

In spite of the fact that it's owned by Microsoft, it's available for both Mac and Windows, so there's no problem using it if you have team members on different platforms.

OneDrive also has a feature that I've found incredibly helpful and that is that Skype is built into it. I love this because I can send a quick Skype message to a team member or start a quick text, video or voice chat while I'm working on documents without ever leaving OneDrive.

Another feature that it has that is lacking in Google Drive is OneNote [Ref 39]. I love the desktop version of OneNote. The online version found in OneDrive is a stripped-down version that I don't like nearly as much as the desktop version, but it has the basic features you really need. If you're a "notebooky" kind of person and you want to share your notebooks with team members, OneDrive may be a better option for you than Google Drive.

OneDrive also comes with a terabyte of free storage with many Office365 [Ref 40] subscriptions, and has the same file sharing options that you'll find in Google Drive.

For the reasons listed above, I switched from Google Drive to OneDrive.

For the most part I've been happy with the decision to switch from Google Drive to OneDrive, but there is one big drawback, and that is that OneDrive isn't as popular as Google Drive and because of that, it doesn't integrate with as many programs.

Since the two programs are similar, I'd encourage you to experiment with both to see which one you like best.

EVERNOTE

Evernote [Ref 41] and OneNote are two very similar programs. OneNote is more robust than Evernote, but Evernote is very popular and due to its popularity integrates with more programs than OneNote.

Rebecca Livermore

Like OneNote, Evernote also has sharing capabilities, so if a notebook style of organizing your content appeals to you, check it out.

If you decide to use OneDrive instead of an option such as Google Drive, then I recommend using OneNote. If you decide to go with Google Drive, Evernote may be a better option for you.

DROPBOX

Dropbox [Ref 42] is an extremely popular file sharing option. You can upload files of all types including videos, Word documents, Excel spreadsheets, images, and audio files, and then share those files with your team members.

I used to use Dropbox all the time, but moved away from it after getting into Google Drive and OneDrive. The reason that I made the switch is because you can't do actual document creation in Dropbox. You can only upload files that you've already created. You also cannot collaborate in real time in documents in Dropbox, and in fact, if you have multiple people work on the same documents, you may end up with more than one version of a document.

One other downside to Dropbox is that if you share a lot of folders with other team members, it takes up space not just in your Dropbox account, but in theirs as well. If you share a smaller number of files and/or if you don't share a lot of large files, this won't be a problem. But if you share a lot of files or files such as videos, you and your team members will end up needing pro accounts. Your team members may already have paid versions of Dropbox, but if they don't and if the files you share with them requires them to upgrade, this is an expense you should cover for them.

On the plus side, due to its popularity, Dropbox integrates with many other programs.

PRIVATE YOUTUBE VIDEOS

If you've created a lot of training videos and don't want to upload them to Google Drive or OneDrive, you can upload them to YouTube and make them private.

It's important to understand the difference between private videos and unlisted videos. Private videos can only be viewed by people you've specifically shared them with. In contrast, unlisted videos can be viewed by anyone with the link to the video.

It's easiest to select "unlisted" as the option for videos that you want to share with your team because then it's unnecessary to go in and give new team members permission to view the videos. If you use the unlisted option rather than the private option, you can add links to your unlisted videos to the procedures you create, and the links will work, regardless of who clicks on them.

The downside, of course, is that since anyone with the link can view the videos, it's possible for them to be shared with people outside your team.

The best way to deal with this is to make videos unlisted if you're not overly concerned about who sees them, and make them private if you want to ensure that only specific people have access to them

If you use multiple Google products such as Gmail, Google Calendar and Google Drive to collaborate with your team, using private or unlisted YouTube videos is a great way to share training videos with your team. This is due to the fact that YouTube is owned by Google, so it is available from within the Google dashboard, which makes it a convenient option for heavy Google users.

LASTPASS

Many business owners are reluctant to share passwords with team members. But often times in order for someone to do his job, he must have your passwords.

Rebecca Livermore

LastPass [Ref 43] is a great program that allows you to share your passwords with team members without them ever actually seeing the passwords. When you change your passwords, simply update them in LastPass and your team members will immediately have access to the new passwords without having to ask.

You can also quickly remove permissions to access your various accounts should a team member stop working for you.

LastPass is a convenient and secure way to share passwords with your team. It's available for both Mac and Windows, and has both a free and premium option.

A Healthy Team is a Productive Team

UNFORTUNATELY, RELATIONSHIPS CAN BE complicated. What may start off as a good relationship can go south if the relationship isn't properly nourished. We see this in personal relationships all too often. The husband and wife who promise "till death do us part" at the altar may later call it quits and file for divorce. Friends part ways over big and sometimes small things, and family members become estranged.

While there are a lot of dynamics in personal relationships that don't carry over into business relationships, human emotion is at the heart of every relationship, regardless of whether the relationship is personal or business oriented.

This section will help you navigate the sometimes-complex human emotions that can impact the health of your team.

Rebecca Livermore

Chapter 31

The Golden Rule Never Goes Out of Style

If you ask people what the Golden Rule is, you may get more than one answer. Some people say that it means that "he who has the gold rules." Others use the Golden Rule to mean that you should treat others the way you want to be treated.

Unfortunately, some business owners use the first definition, and since they are the ones with the "gold" they take on the posture of being the ruler. Sadly, if you focus on being the ruler because you are the one paying people, you may end up with an unhealthy team.

Now it's true that as the business owner, you are the leader, but one aspect of effective leadership, especially if you want your team to be healthy, is to treat others the way you want to be treated.

While it may seem that you're giving up a lot by this approach, in the long run your team will function better if you use Golden Rule thinking in the management of your team.

Here are a few ways to go about that.

Pay What You Would Want to Be Paid

Managing a tight financial ship is important, if you want your blog and business to be profitable. But it's not cool to be as cheap as possible.

Yes, you may opt to hire workers from the Philippines because you can do so cheaper than you can if you stick with hiring people in the U.S. There's nothing wrong with that. But if you hire team members from the Philippines, you should pay them what is considered a good wage there.

If you hire American workers, start them at the going rate for the duties they perform. If they are independent contractors, pay them at a higher hourly rate than you would an employee. The reason for this is simple: you won't have to cover the same costs as you would for employees. For instance, you likely won't provide office space, computers, health insurance and other things that you would for employees. The independent contractor must pay for all of these things herself. Independent contractors also only get paid for the work they actually do, and aren't paid for unbillable hours which include things like reading email, bookkeeping, learning new programs, etc.

As a former independent contractor, I found that only about half of my work day was spent on billable hours.

Also, as your business prospers, reward those who work for you. For example, if you have a big launch and people had to work really hard to help you out with it, give them a bonus. If your team members' skills increase give them a pay raise. If they work for you long term, reward their faithfulness with bonuses and pay raises.

The key thing is to ask yourself if you would want someone to be stingy with you. Since the answer to that is likely no, then don't be stingy with your team members!

LET GO OF SUPER VA EXPECTATIONS

Chris Ducker has written a lot about the Super VA syndrome [Ref 44]. The basic idea is expecting a single team member to be good at everything.

It's easy to lapse into this thinking if you want to keep things simple, not to mention if you don't have the finances to hire multiple team members.

No one is good at everything and expecting that of your team members will not only frustrate them. It will also set them up for failure.

Instead of expecting someone to be good at everything, before hiring them, find out what they consider to be their strengths and weaknesses. Avoid hiring someone who claims to be good at everything! Even a person with multiple talents will have shortcomings.

If someone claims to be good at multiple things, dig a bit deeper to find out what they really enjoy doing. (Chances are, if they really enjoy it, they'll also be good at it.) For instance, if someone claims to be a great writer and also great at bookkeeping, ask which of the two they most enjoy, and focus their tasks on that. Resort to using them in the less desirable areas only when absolute necessary and only on a temporary basis.

GIVE CREDIT WHERE CREDIT IS DUE

When I was still doing client work, I was content to mostly stay in the background. I didn't blab about what I did for others, and didn't secretly long to have my name and accomplishments broadcasted. In spite of that, I did appreciate it when I was publicly praised for the work I did.

While it's best to publicly give credit for the work that others do, it's okay to be quiet about it as well. However, one thing that is wrong 100% of the time is to claim that an idea was yours or to take credit for work that was actually done by someone else.

Rebecca Livermore

I once did a major project for a client that took months of work. The initial concept was mine, all of the research on it was mine, and the entire process for it was something I created. Receiving public credit for the work never crossed my mind, but I was shocked when this person publicly took credit for the idea, and in fact went out of his way to go on stage and tell people how he came up with the idea.

I felt betrayed, and the trust in the relationship was broken as a result of him taking credit for my idea and all the hard work I did.

Chapter 32

KEEPING THE LINES OF COMMUNICATION OPEN

A LOT OF HEARTACHE, CONFLICT AND CONFUSION can be avoided if the lines of communication are kept open.

While you don't want to spend an excessive amount of time on communication, regular communication can contribute to the overall health of your team.

Below are some of the tools that I've used both in my work for clients as well as with my own team members.

UBERCONFERENCE

Uberconference [Ref 45] is a free conference call option that is quick and easy to use. While there is a free version, I chose to go with the pro version since among other things, no pin number is needed for the meetings.

With Uberconference, your team members can keep the conference line phone number in the address book on their phones and with a single click, join a team meeting.

Uberconference has a recording option as well, and allows screensharing via the web. I've found it to be a great option for team

Rebecca Livermore

meetings, and as an added bonus, I can use it with clients as well, and can also use it to provide teleseminars.

SKYPE

Skype [Ref 46] is great for video chats. One thing that I love about it is that it's free, and as long as people have an Internet connection, they can use it from anywhere in the world.

It's an especially great option if you use OneDrive for your document sharing and storage since you can start conversations with your team from within the same dashboard where all of your files are located.

SLACK

Slack [Ref 47]is a relatively new kid on the block, and it's quickly gaining momentum. It has both free and paid options. For most small teams, the free option is more than sufficient.

Slack is a great way to reduce the amount of email that goes back and forth, since much of the communication on an item can be done via Slack, rather than email.

You can set up channels that pertain to different aspects of your blog, and keep all communication related to a specific topic in one channel. For example, you may have a channel for your podcast, a different channel for written content and another channel for graphics. You can share channels with just the people on your team who need access.

You can also have private communication with individual team members on an as-needed basis.

If you feel overwhelmed by email, Slack is a tool worth looking into.

EMAIL

Love it or hate it, to some degree email is here to stay. However, since it's easy for emails to get buried, I don't recommend it as a primary communication tool. Instead, try one of the other options such as Skype or Slack for your primary communication tool and use email only when necessary.

TEXTING

Texting is great for time-sensitive communication. Personally, since your team members likely work for multiple clients, I recommend avoiding texting unless something truly is time sensitive. For instance, if you sent a time sensitive email and your team member didn't respond quickly, you may want to send a text to alert them to the email.

Rebecca Livermore

When (Not If) Things Go Wrong

SOMETIMES THINGS GO WRONG. That's a simple fact of life that applies to everything, including teams. Because of that, it's important to plan for it so that you'll handle things well when the need to deal with problems arises.

In this section, I'll cover how to let someone go when needed, but before I go into that, I want to talk about the importance of managing expectations. This is important because most, if not all, of the conflict in relationships is a result of unmet expectations. You may expect your team members to know or do certain things, and when they don't, you may be disappointed, frustrated and perhaps even angry.

By the same token, your team members may have their own expectations and when you fail to meet them, they may become disillusioned and quit, or even worse, start an "attitude attack" that spreads throughout your team.

For both reasons, it's important to always keep expectations front and center and communicate about them on a regular basis.

With that in mind, let's dive into Fire-able Offenses, and how to deal with growing pains on your team.

Rebecca Livermore

Chapter 33

FIRE-ABLE OFFENSES

IT'S OFTEN BEEN SAID THAT YOU SHOULD hire slow and fire fast. While I'm all for hiring slow, firing fast can be a bit harsh. I do agree with that advice if shortly after hiring someone you realize that they simply aren't a good fit.

To avoid having to fire people, consider initially hiring them for a small project or a series of small projects before making them a more permanent part of your team. This can be one way to hire slow.

Once you've hired someone as a more permanent part of your team, it's important in my opinion to do your best to give them the same chance to make things right as you would want if you were in their position.

Having said that, there are a few things that should be considered fire-able offenses, even without a lot of warning. For example, if a team member steals from you, it's not out of line to immediately terminate them. Or perhaps they publicly bad-mouthed you. Those and other things that only you can determine can rightly fit into the "fire fast" category.

KEEP SHORT ACCOUNTS

Rebecca Livermore

In all relationships, including both business and personal, it's important to keep short accounts. Don't let things fester. If something bothers you, let the person know. Likewise, if you sense that a team member is upset with you, don't wait for them to bring it up. Shoot straight with them. Let them know that you sense they are upset with you and ask if that's the case, and if so, what you can do to make things right.

Make a point of fostering a safe work environment where people can be honest about their struggles without worrying about being fired.

Obviously, their respect is important, and if a team member is disrespectful on a regular basis, it may be time to part ways. But don't immediately shut people down if they're frustrated and just blowing off steam.

ACCEPT BLAME

There's nothing worse than blaming things that go wrong on other people, when the cause of a problem is at least partly your responsibility.

When things go wrong, admit your part in them. If a team member is frustrated with you, even if their frustration and criticism seems unjust, look for the kernel of truth, and make adjustments as needed.

HOW TO LET SOMEONE GO GRACEFULLY

In spite of all of your efforts to hire well, communicate well, and admit your own mistakes, there may come a time when you simply need to let someone go.

Depending on your relationship with them and whether or not they could really jeopardize your blog and business if they're disgruntled, when possible, give as much notice to someone as you can.

This isn't always possible, because when it's time to part ways, things may be tense, and the potential may exist for the person to do things that impact you, your other team members, and your entire blog and business in a negative way.

If that's the case, consider immediate termination, but provide some level of severance pay if you have the means to do so. For example, you may let them go immediately (and immediately cut off all access to your accounts), but give them one-month's pay to help them in their transition.

If it is just a matter of the person not being a good fit for you, but someone that you may recommend to others, write up a letter of recommendation, or leave them a positive recommendation on LinkedIn. You may even want to introduce them to others in your circle that you do feel would be a good match for them.

Say as much as is needed to other team members about your decision to let the person go, but never more than is needed. Remember to once again practice the golden rule by putting yourself in the shoes of the other person and treating him like you'd want to be treated if the roles were reversed.

Rebecca Livermore

Chapter 34

GROWING PAINS

THERE MAY BE TIMES WHEN IT'S NECESSARY for a team member to move on due to growing pains – either yours or theirs – sometimes both. For instance, as your blog grows, you may need someone to work more hours than you initially hired her for. Slight increases in hours may be welcome, but if the demand is more than the person can handle, it may be necessary for you to part ways.

Likewise, the person's own business may be growing in a way that they can no longer accommodate you, as they want to put more time into their own content.

While I put this in the section on what to do when things go wrong, it's important to understand that growing pains aren't necessarily a bad thing. As your business grows, you may become too big for some of your best team members. On top of that, if you hire real talent, they will likely keep growing and at some point, may have gone as far as they can with you, and need to move on.

Even though it's likely a good thing, change is often painful, even when good. The suggestions below can help ease this type of transition.

HAVE A TRANSITION AGREEMENT WITH KEY PLAYERS

Rebecca Livermore

I had an agreement in place with one of my former clients. I worked a lot of hours for her, and because of that, what she paid me was the bulk of my income. I would have been in bad shape had the relationship been terminated with no notice for whatever reason. Likewise, since I did as much as I did for her, she would have been in a bad place had I quit with only a two-week notice. Because of that, when we together decided to increase my hours, we agreed that if either of us decided it was time for me to move on that we would give a two-month, rather than a two-week notice.

The time finally came for that to happen, and the longer notice helped both of us to transition well. This wouldn't work in every working relationship, but it's a good thing to consider with any key players on your team.

PROVIDE REFERENCES AND MAKE INTRODUCTIONS

Assuming that you were happy with the person's work, provide references for them, write letters of recommendation, testimonials, LinkedIn recommendations, or anything else that they need to move on to bigger and better things.

ASSIST EACH OTHER IN FUTURE PROJECTS

Just because you stop working together in your previous capacity doesn't mean that you can't still assist each other on some level. For instance, in the relationship that I referred to above, I've been able to give input on certain aspects of content creation, and she has helped me out in various ways as well.

Regardless of what you do, when it's time to move on, don't burn any bridges. You never know when you may need to connect again in some capacity. And never, ever publicly say negative things about the person, regardless of the circumstances.

Conclusion

WE'VE COME TO THE END OF THIS EXPLORATION of what it may look like for you, as a blogger, to work with a team. While this book has come to an end, hopefully the journey for you as a team-leading blogger is anything but ending. It's time to embrace team members, however big or small the tasks may be.

The main thing is to start. Start with small tasks, and add bigger tasks and more team members as your blog and business grow. Embrace how others can enhance your blog and other aspects of your business. Never stop growing, and never stop learning.

Your blog will indeed grow faster and better with the help of a team.

I wish you the best on the journey.

Happy blogging!

Rebecca Livermore

My Gift to You

Thank you again for purchasing this book. Regardless of what else you do; your blog won't be successful if you don't blog consistently. Since that struggle is real, I want to encourage you to download The Five Secrets to Developing the Blogging Habit. I've made it available to you absolutely free.

To get your complimentary eCourse delivered right to your inbox all you have to do is visit

http://professionalcontentcreation.com/blogginghabit

Rebecca Livermore

References

[Ref 1]: The curse of knowledge is when you know something so well, you assume everyone else knows what it means and fail to explain it.

[Ref 2]: Content Repurposing Made Easy is a book and course that I created. You can check it out here:
http://ProfessionalContentCreation.com/CRME

[Ref 3]: The Sales Lion
http://thesaleslion.com

[Ref 4]: Chris Ducker's 3 Lists to Freedom
http://www.chrisducker.com/3-lists-to-freedom/

[Ref 5]: 1 Day Business Breakthrough
https://1daybb.com

[Ref 6]: Profit First by Mike Michalowicz
http://www.profitfirstbook.com/

[Ref 7]: AWeber, email marketing
ProfessionalContentCreation.com/AWeber

[Ref 8]: GetResponse email marketing (this is what I personally use)
ProfessionalContentCreation.com/GetResponse

[Ref 9]: SlideShare is a site where you can upload slide decks created with PowerPoint, Keynote, etc. It's a great way to repurpose your blog content. You can use it to drive traffic back to your blog, promote your products, etc. Here's an example of a SlideShare presentation that the contractor I hired did for me: http://www.slideshare.net/ProContentCreation/how-to-create-a-podcast-with-great-sound-without-breaking-the-bank

[Ref 10]: Google Plus Communities
https://plus.google.com/communities

[Ref 11]: Slack
https://slack.com

[Ref 12]: Google Drive
http://drive.google.com

[Ref 13]: The Definitive Guide to Paying Home-Based Filipino Virtual Assistants by Chris Ducker
http://www.chrisducker.com/how-much-do-i-pay-my-virtual-assistant/

[Ref 14]: Priority VA is a small, U.S. based virtual assistant agency that has a good mix of personal attention coupled with some of the perks of working through an agency.
http://priorityva.com

[Ref 15] Fancy Hands plans start at $29.99 per month. Tasks must take no longer than 15 minutes, and you don't have a dedicated assistant.
http://fancyhands.com

[Ref 16] WPCurve is an affordable way to get ongoing technical support for your WordPress site. At the current time, pricing starts at $79 per month for unlimited 30-minute tasks.
https://wpcurve.com/

[Ref 17]: Virtual Staff Finder
http://www.virtualstafffinder.com/

[Ref 18]: OnlineJobs.Ph

http://OnlineJobs.Ph

[Ref 19]: Fiverr
http://Fiverr.com
[Ref 20]: Evernote
http://Evernote.com

[Ref 21]: OneNote
http://www.onenote.com/

[Ref 22]: Twitter Lists
https://support.twitter.com/articles/76460

[Ref 23:]: Feedly
http://feedly.com

[Ref 24]: Edgar
http://meetedgar.com/

[Ref 25]: Buffer
http://bufferapp.com

[Ref 26]: Facebook Ads training – Jon Loomer has both free and paid training on Facebook ads that is excellent. Here are a couple of links to get you started:
http://www.jonloomer.com/phc/
http://www.jonloomer.com/search/ads

[Ref 27]: Canva – a great and easy-to-use tool for creating images.
http://Canva.com

[Ref 28]: PicMonkey – another great free tool for creating images. There is both a free and paid version. The paid version is only about $5 per month and is well worth it. This is my personal favorite tool for creating images.
http://professionalcontentcreation.com/picmonkey

[Ref 29]: Pixlr – Pixlr is a free tool with "Photoshop like" features. There is also an express version that is a very easy to use tool for creating images.
http://pixlr.com

[Ref 30]: Jing – Jing is a free tool that you can use to create screencast videos and annotated screengrabs.
https://www.techsmith.com/jing.html

[Ref 31]: Snagit – Snagit is a step up from Jing. It's a good mid-level program for creating and editing screencast videos, and images.
https://www.techsmith.com/snagit.html

[Ref 32]: Screenflow – Screenflow is the screen recording tool of choice for many Mac users.
https://itunes.apple.com/us/app/screenflow-5/id917790450?mt=12

[Ref 33]: Camtasia – Very similar to Screenflow, but available for both Mac and Windows. The Windows version is more robust.
https://www.techsmith.com/camtasia.html

[Ref 34]: Sweet Process – this is a great tool for documenting your processes.
http://www.sweetprocess.com/

[Ref 35]: Lynda –when it comes to computer and tech training this is probably the best video tutorial site on the web.
http://professionalcontentcreation.com/lynda

[Ref 36]: Udemy – also a great place to learn all kind of things. One thing I like about Udemy compared to Lynda is that with Udemy, you purchase individual courses and have lifetime access to them, rather than paying a monthly fee like you have to with Lynda.
http://udemy.com

[Ref 37]: Google Drive
http://drive.google.com

[Ref 38]: OneDrive
http://OneDrive.live.com

[Ref 39]: OneNote
http://onenote.com

[Ref 40]: Office365
https://products.office.com/en-us/business/explore-office-365-for-business

[Ref 41]: Evernote
http://evernote.com

[Ref 42]: Dropbox
http://Dropbox.com

[Ref 43]: LastPass
http://lastpass.com

[Ref 44]: Chris Ducker's post, Debunking the 'Super VA' Myth – Why ONE Virtual Assistant Can't Do It All!
http://www.chrisducker.com/debunking-the-super-va-myth/

[Ref 45]: Uberconference – the tool I use for conference calls.
http://uberconference.com

[Ref 46]: Skype
http://www.skype.com/en/

[Ref 47]: Slack
https://slack.com/

Rebecca Livermore

Other Books by Rebecca Livermore

You can find my entire catalog of books here:

http://professionalcontentcreation.com/books

Thank you for checking out my other books!

About the Author

Rebecca Livermore is a bestselling author, blogger, and the owner of Professional Content Creation, a company focused on helping business owners use content to market their businesses. She has worked as a freelance writer since 1993 and has served as a content manager for top bloggers such as Michael Hyatt, Amy Porterfield, and Marcus Sheridan. Her passion is helping others integrate faith and business in their blogs, books and all other aspects of content creation.

She has been married to her husband, Chuck, for more than 30 years and is the mother of two young adults who affectionately nicknamed her, "Hot Rod Mama."

www.ingramcontent.com/pod-product-compliance
Lightning Source LLC
Chambersburg PA
CBHW022038190326
41520CB00008B/628